| DATE | | |
|---|---|---|
| | | |
| | | |
| | | |
| | | |
| | | |
| | | |
| | | |
| | | |
| | | |
| | | |
| | | |
| | | |
| | | |

# DIGGING UP THE PAST

SIR LEONARD WOOLLEY

# DIGGING UP THE PAST

**GREENWOOD PRESS, PUBLISHERS**
WESTPORT, CONNECTICUT

Library of Congress Cataloging in Publication Data

Woolley, Charles Leonard, Sir, 1880-1960.
    Digging up the past.

    Reprint of the 2d ed. published in 1954 by
Benn, London.
    Includes index.
    1.  Archaeology--Methodology.  2.  Excavations
(Archaeology)  I.  Title.
[CC76.W66  1977]        930'.1'028        77-13325
ISBN 0-8371-9853-4

First Edition  1930
Second Edition  1954

Reprinted with the permission of Ernest Benn Limited

Reprinted in 1977 by Greenwood Press, Inc.,
51 Riverside Avenue, Westport, CT. 06880

Printed in the United States of America

# PREFACE TO THE SECOND EDITION

THIS BOOK WAS FIRST PUBLISHED IN 1930 and when the publishers proposed that in this edition it should be brought up to date I imagined that to do so after a lapse of nearly a quarter of a century would involve a great deal of work. Actually this has not been the case. If I had been dealing with the results of field archæology most of the chapters would have had to be re-written, for in almost every field the last twenty years have seen so great an advance in our knowledge that there are few conclusions arrived at in the 1920's which do not need modification to-day—the facts remain, but they have to be re-interpreted in the light of new facts. But *Digging up the Past* dealt with principles and methods, and these change little if at all. I had not, in those early days, said a great deal about the use of air photography, which has become one of the most potent weapons of field archæology, but writers far more qualified than I, such as O. G. S. Crawford, have written fully on the subject, and I can perhaps plead that since it

is not so much a part of digging as a preliminary to it I may be excused from quoting them
at length. There are now new methods of
dating objects, by dendrochronology and by
the radioactivity of carbon; however useful
they may prove they have nothing to do with
digging as such; the digger may supply the
material but it is for the scientist in his laboratory to practise the method. The additions
which I have made are all in character with
the book as originally written, the purpose of
which was to explain to the layman the kind of
work that the field archæologist does and why
he does it. Some necessary aspects of that work
I have merely referred to in passing—for
instance, the writing of field notes and the
cataloguing of objects—partly because they can
be taken for granted, partly because every
excavator employs—or should employ—the
system which best suits himself and there is no
hard-and-fast formula to be generally observed;
we make our notes, each of us, for our own use,
and the particular form which they take is of
no interest to anyone else. I have tried throughout to make it clear that archæology is a very
human science; if we constrict the archæologist
in the strait-waistcoat of what has been called
'methodology' he will be only too apt to lose

that human element which is the sole justification of his being.  Of course, objects must be catalogued and the catalogue must record measurements and material, form, colour, technique and, perhaps, chemical composition; but never forget that the object was made by an individual man who was not bothering about any such analysis but was a creator giving shape to an idea.  The archæologist's job is to get through the object to its maker; if he does that then, helped by the material qualities of the thing, he will begin to understand the society in which the thing's maker lived.  Anybody can dig up things; but it is only by observation and interpretation that we can dig up the past.

L.W.

# CONTENTS

# ILLUSTRATIONS

(Photographs of the Ur Excavations are reproduced
by courtesy of the Trustees of the British Museum and
of the Museum of the University of Pennsylvania.)

xi

## NOTE

This little book is based on a series of six talks broadcast by the B.B.C., to whom I am indebted for permission to re-publish the substance in permanent form.

## Chapter I

## Introductory

BEFORE I BEGIN TO DESCRIBE THE METHODS of Field Archæology it might be as well to say something about its aims. Nobody supposes that the digging up of antiquities is in itself a scientific end, and though there is always a thrill attending the discovery of buried treasure the ever-growing interest of the public in archæological work is by no means limited to its dramatic accidents; behind the mere romance there is something of real and enduring value.

It is difficult at first to get in proper perspective such discoveries as those of Tutankhamen's tomb, of the Palace of Minos in Crete and of the royal tombs at Ur; isolated by their novelty they come out of focus and dazzle us, but later they withdraw and, linking up with other things in the field of ordered vision, become features in the historical background against which, consciously or unconsciously, we play our part. When Schliemann found the treasures of Mycenæ what first startled the world was his belief that Homer's poems had been proved to be literally true : now few would argue whether or not in those tombs lay the bodies of Agamemnon and Clytemnestra masked with gold, but no one thinks of Homer or of the beginnings of Greek history without having at the back of his mind the picture of Mycenæan pomp and beauty.

In these days natural science is unfolding before us a panorama which to our great-grandfathers seemed in its beginnings blasphemous : to them it undermined the foundations of belief, to us it establishes thought upon a base broader and more rational. Science reckons time in millions of years and stretches space to infinity; the wider outlook does not make us one bit less interested in the things of to-day and to-morrow, and may seem scarcely to affect our practice, but it is there, part of our consciousness, and the more it is explored the better we can understand ourselves. Archæology is doing the same thing in a smaller field : it deals with a period limited to a few thousand years and its subject is not the universe, not even the human race, but modern man. We dig, and say of these pots and pans, these beads and weapons, that they date back to

3000 or 4000 B.C., and the onlooker is tempted to exclaim at their age, and to admire them simply because they are old. Their real interest lies in the fact that they are new. If mere age be the standard, all that we unearth is insignificant compared to the dinosaur's fossil egg, and, for that matter, what is six thousand years in the life of the human race when we have to calculate that in terms of geological periods? The importance of our archæological material is that it throws light on the history of men very like ourselves, on a civilization which is bound up with that of to-day.

We cannot divorce ourselves from our past: we are always conscious of precedents, not least so when we flout them, and we let experience shape our views and actions: this is so much the case that when tradition is absent or crystallizes into unreasoned convention, as it has done with the Australian Bushmen, progress stops. But the past to which we appeal must be in a sense our own, precedents set by men conditioned much as we are, the experience of races or individuals morally akin to us; its value is proportionate to the degree of continuity by which we are linked to it.

The political thinker of a hundred years ago would cite his parallels and draw his arguments from the Roman or Greek world, finding that cognate with his own, but there he stopped short; Greek civilization presented itself to him as something born full-grown with no history behind it, giving little opportunity for observing development and cause. To-day we can see that modern man did not begin his career in 500 B.C., not even perhaps in 5000 B.C.; from the flower of Attic culture we can work back and find the roots spreading far afield, and sending up perennial blossoms all differing with the nature of the soil and the tending they have received, but all of one stock, and in the light of such knowledge we can better judge and control the present and the future growth. And this enlightenment is not merely for the specialist, for the research student in history. The opening-up of the world affects us all, becomes part of the general intellectual inheritance, and the justification of archæ-ology is that it does in the end concern every-one. Its direct appeal is due to the fact that, compared with natural science, it comes with simpler introductions. Its subject is modern man, not a universe which resolves itself more and more into an intellectual abstraction, and its material is the work of man's hands. We see the elaborate drainage-system of Knossos

PLATE I

Clearing graves, Ur

(See p. 95)

PLATE II

The so-called 'Antioch Chalice'

(Reproduced from 'The Great Chalice of Antioch' by Gustavus A. Eisen.
International Copyright by the publishers, Kouchakji Freres, New York)

(*See p.* 8)

and at once feel at home; the cosmetics found in an ancient grave strike us as pathetically up to date; the surprise which a visitor to a museum expresses at the age of a given object is in exact proportion to his recognition of the object's essential modernity—it is the surprise of one who sees his horizon suddenly opening out; and the advantage of archæology is that it offers Darien peaks so many and so easy to climb.

I was led to write the above by being told that the first question which the reader would like to have answered might be, 'Why does anyone dig?' and that came as a shock, for it had seemed to me so obvious that the purpose of archæology is to illustrate and to discover the course of human civilization, which is certainly an end worth while. But it might be urged that the question is specifically confined to Field Archæology, whereas the course of civilization is the subject of History: that being so, if the historian uses as his material those relics of the past which the field archæologist does, as a matter of fact, bring to light, could not the material be produced by casual digging? Is there any justification for a person who claims to be an expert in a specialized branch of science and then does in an elaborate way what the labourer could do much more cheaply?

If that is what the question means—and it could mean a good many things—it betrays complete ignorance of what Field Archæology is. In its essence Field Archæology is the application of scientific method to the excavation of ancient objects, and it is based on the theory that the historical value of an object depends not so much on the nature of the object itself as on its associations, which only scientific excavation can detect. The casual digger and the plunderer aim at getting something of artistic or commercial value, and there their interest stops. The archæologist, being after all human, does enjoy finding rare and beautiful objects, but wants to know all about them, and in any case prefers the acquisition of knowledge to that of things; for him digging consists very largely in observation, recording and interpretation. There is all the difference in the world between the purpose and the methods of the scientific worker and those of the robber; it remains to be seen whether there is a corresponding difference in the value of the work done. Really the whole of this book is an attempt to explain the means which the archæologist adopts, and to prove that they do achieve the end in view, but it may be as well to clear the ground in advance by showing to how great an extent the historical value of an object depends on our knowledge of the conditions in which it was found.

Supposing that a peasant somewhere or other unearths a marble statue or a gold ornament; he sells it, and it passes from hand to hand until from a dealer's shop it makes its way into a museum or a private collection. By this time nobody knows where it was found or how, it has been torn from its context and can be judged only as a thing in itself; its quality as a work of art does not suffer, but how about its historical value? Experts have to guess, from such knowledge as they already possess, to what country and age it belongs, and, if they agree, the statue or cup is assumed to illustrate further that particular known phase of art; very likely they will not agree, and it becomes merely a bone of contention for the learned, and a source of confusion for the layman. If the object found be, for instance, a clay pot having no claim to artistic merit, then, stripped of any significance it might have possessed as a historical document, it becomes absolutely valueless; if the finding of an important object be incorrectly reported it becomes a positive stumbling-block to science.   Some Arabs, digging in the ruins of a Syrian church, discover by chance a silver goblet adorned with figures in relief, amongst them some which can credibly be identified as Christ and his apostles.   Through various hands it passes to America.   The dealers are ready with the story that it was discovered at Antioch, and 'the disciples were called Christians first at Antioch'; and the world is assured that here is the Holy Grail, the actual chalice of the Last Supper, bearing contemporary portraits of the apostles (*see* Plate II); though the goblet was, in fact, found more than a hundred miles away from Antioch, and though, judging from its style, it must have been made at least three hundred years after Christ's death, it is hard to dispel an error which has already gained a hearing and has so dramatic a ring.   In this particular case the harm done to science was less because the story told was demonstrably false, and the purpose of it was clearly interested; many people might be deceived, but the expert was not obliged to re-cast his knowledge, gained from innumerable dated objects, of the art of the first four Christian centuries; but where the background of definite knowledge is slight an object robbed of its context may be a snare even to the expert. I recall the case of a bronze figure of a lion purchased in China; presumably it was Chinese, but to a certain scholar it seemed to present analogies with the very few such monuments that we possess of Hittite art; he declared it to be Hittite, and then made it the criterion for judging other works of art whose Hittite origin could not be disputed. Here subjective criticism based on too partial knowledge was to blame, but had anything been recorded as to the conditions of the lion's finding we should have been spared so much confusion in the history of Near Eastern art.

On the other hand an object of no value in itself may become a historical document of the greatest importance just because its associations have been properly observed. The great stone ruins of Zimbabwe, in Rhodesia, had long been a puzzle, and the wildest theories were current about them—they had been built by the Phœnicians, they were the Ophir from which Solomon obtained his gold, they were an outpost of ancient Egypt; and observe that if any one of these theories had been proved correct we should have had to revise very thoroughly our views of ancient history. A worthless scrap of Chinese porcelain found in the foundations of

the building, but found in the course of a
scientific excavation properly controlled, proves
that the so-called temple is mediæval in date,
and must be native African in authorship. A
speculator digging for profit would never have
bothered about that little potsherd nor, if he
had, would anyone have paid any attention to
it, for the very good reason that his methods
would not have been such that his discoveries
could have been accepted as scientific evidence:
found as it was, it not only knocked falsehood
on the head but opened up a new chapter in
African history.

Treasure-hunting is almost as old as Man;
scientific archæology is a modern development,
but in its short life of about seventy years it has
done marvels. Thanks to excavation, thousands
of years of human history are now familiar
which a hundred years ago were a total blank,
but this is not all, perhaps not even the most
important part. The old histories, resting
principally on written documents, were largely
confined to those events which at every age
writers thought most fit to record—wars,
political happenings, the chronicles of kings—
with such side-lights as could be gleaned from
the literature of the time. The digger may
produce more written records, but he also

brings to light a mass of objects illustrating the arts and handicrafts of the past, the temples in which men worshipped, the houses in which they lived, the setting in which their lives were spent; he supplies the material for a social history of a sort that could never have been undertaken before. Until Schliemann dug at Mycenæ, and Sir Arthur Evans in Crete, no one guessed that there had been a Minoan civilization. Not a single written word has been found to tell of it, yet we can trace the rise and fall of the ancient Minoan power, can see again the splendours of the Palace of Minos, and imagine how life was lived alike there and in the crowded houses of the humbler folk. The whole history of Egypt has been recovered by archæ-ological work, and that in astonishing detail; I suppose we know more about ordinary life in Egypt in the fourteenth century before Christ than we do about that of England in the fourteenth century A.D. To the spade we owe our knowledge of the Sumerians and the Hittites, great empires whose very existence had been forgotten, and in the case of other ancient peoples, the Babylonians and the Assyrians, the dry bones of previously known fact have had life breathed into them by the excavation of buried sites. It is a fine list of achievements, and it might be greatly expanded; all over Europe, in Central America, in China and in Turkestan excavation is supplementing our knowledge, and adding new vistas to our outlook over man's past; and to what is it all due? Not to the mere fact that antique objects have been dug out of the ground, but to their having been dug out scientifically.

But before I describe methods there is another point arising out of that first question 'Why does anyone dig?' People sometimes put the accent in a different place, and ask 'Why does anyone *dig*? Why do they have to use the spade to achieve these admirable results? How does it come about that things get buried and have to be dug up?'

Clearly, in the case of graves, which yield many of the archæologist's treasures, the question does not arise, for the things were put underground deliberately and have remained there; but how do houses and cities sink below the earth's surface? They do not: the earth rises above them, and though people do not recognize the fact, it is happening all around them every day. Go no further than London. How many steps does one have to go down to enter the Temple Church? Yet it stood origin-

PLATE III

Air photograph of the Roman town of Caistor, before excavation
The lines of streets and buildings can be seen clearly
*(Royal Air Force Official—Crown Copyright reserved)*

*(See p.* 18)

PLATE IV

The basket-men at work.  A long climb to the waggons, Ur

(*See p.* 30)

ally at ground level. The mosaic pavements of Roman Londinium lie twenty-five to thirty feet below the streets of the modern City. Wherever a place has been continuously occupied the same thing has happened. In old times municipal scavenging did not amount to much, the street was the natural receptacle for refuse and the street level gradually rose with accumulated filth; if it was re-paved the new cobbles were laid over the old dirt, at a higher level, and you stepped down into the houses on either side. When a house was pulled down and rebuilt the site would be partly filled in, and the new ground floor set at or above street level; the foundations of the older building would remain undisturbed below ground. The process would be repeated time after time so that when foundations are made for the huge buildings of to-day which go down nearly as far into the earth as they rise into the air, the excavating gangs cut through layer after layer of wall stumps and artificial filling of which each represents a stage in the city's growth. In the Near East the rate of rise is faster. The commonest building material is mud brick, and mud brick walls have to be thick; when they collapse the amount of debris is very great and fills the rooms to a considerable height, and as you cannot use mud bricks twice over, and the carting away of rubbish is expensive, the simplest course is to level the surface of the ruins and build on the top of them—which has the further advantage that it raises your new mud-brick building out of reach of the damp. In Syria and in Iraq every village stands on a mound of its own making, and the ruins of an ancient city may rise a hundred feet above the plain, the whole of that hundred feet being composed of superimposed remains of houses, each represented by the foot or so of standing wall which the collapse of the upper part buried and protected from destruction.

But what happens when a site is no longer inhabited?   A Roman camp, for instance, occupied by the legionaries and abandoned after a few years—how does that get buried? Here we have Nature to thank.  I remember how, when the L.C.C. cleared the slum area where Bush House stands to-day, the heaps of broken brickwork and loose mortar were in the following year entirely hidden by a mass of purple willow-herb, and people used to take 'bus rides down the Strand just for the pleasure of looking over the high hoarding at this miracle of wild flowers.  That happened in the space of a few months; had the 'island site' been left undisturbed for as many years, coarse turf would have covered the mounds and the ruins of Booksellers' Row would have been buried like those of Silchester. And if this can happen in the heart of London, how much more so in the country where Nature fights at close range?

I have not mentioned one way in which buildings may be buried, because it is so lamentably rare; that is by volcanic action. If the field archæologist had his will, every ancient capital would have been overwhelmed by the ashes of a conveniently adjacent volcano. It is with a green jealousy that the worker on other sites visits Pompeii and sees the marvellous preservation of its buildings, the houses standing up to the second floor, the frescoes on the walls, and all the furniture and household objects still in their places as the owners left them when they fled from the disaster. Failing a volcano, the best thing that can happen to a city, archæologically speaking, is that it should be sacked and very thoroughly burnt by an enemy. The owners are not in a position to carry anything away and the plunderers are only out after objects intrinsically valuable, the fire will destroy much, but by no means everything, and will bring down on the top of what does remain so much in the way of ashes and broken brickwork that the survivors, if there are any, will not trouble to dig down into the ruins; a burnt site is generally a site undisturbed. It is where cities have decayed slowly that least is to be found in their ruins; the impoverished inhabitants will have pulled down the older buildings to re-use the material in their own hovels, they will make nothing good of their own and they will certainly leave nothing behind them when at last they desert the place; the top levels of such a site generally produce therefore few objects, and not much history except the melancholy history of decadence.

Granted then, that things do get buried in one or other of these ways, how, it may be asked, do you set to work to find them? Why do you dig just where you do?

Burial does not always mean obliteration, and there are generally some surface signs to guide the digger. In the Near East no one could possibly mistake the great mounds or 'tells' which rose above the plain to mark the sites of ancient cities; very often, if the place was an important one, it can be identified from literary sources even before excavation begins; the difficulty is rather, which point of attack to choose in so great an area. In Mesopotamia the highest mound will probably conceal the

PLATE   V

Assessing the day's finds for 'baksheesh,' Ur

(*See p.* 31)

PLATE VI

(a)
(b)
(c)

Archaeological Strata, Ur

(a) A pavement of Cyrus, King of Persia, *circ.* 525 B.C.
(b) A pavement of Nebuchadnezzar, 600 B.C.
(c) Below the pavement, walls of Kurigalzu, 1400 B.C.

(*See p.* 43)

Ziggurat or staged tower attached to the chief temple; sometimes a low-lying patch will betray the position of the temple itself. Herodotus, visiting Egypt in the fifth century B.C., remarked that the temples there always lay in a hollow; the reason was that while the mud-brick houses of the town were short lived and new buildings constructed over the ruins of the old quickly raised the ground-level, the temples, built of stone and kept always in good repair, outlived many generations and remained at the same level throughout; on an Egyptian site, therefore, a square depression ringed about by mounds of crumbling grey brick gives the excavator a very obvious clue. Earthworks are enduring things, and the site, for instance, of a Roman camp in Britain can nearly always be traced by the low grass-clad lines of its ramparts, and the round barrows of the old British dead are still clear to see upon the Downs; but even where there is nothing upstanding, surface indications may not be lacking. In a dry summer the grass withers more quickly where the soil lies thin over the buried tops of stone walls, and I have seen the entire plan of a Roman villa spread out before me where no spade had ever dug; darker lines in a field of growing corn or, in the very early morning, a

3

difference of tone given by the dew on the blades, will show where buildings run underground: nowadays air photographs bring to light evidence invisible to one standing upon the ground. An air photograph gives us the whole layout of the Roman village of Caistor (*see* Plate III), so that the excavator can confidently select the particular building he would like to dig, whereas, before, the site of Caistor was unknown; even more remarkable is it that an air photograph discovered Woodhenge, and showed on the plain surface of ploughed fields the concentric rings of dots where thousands of years ago wooden posts had been planted. From the ground such things are often quite invisible, or visible only at some lucky moment. At Wadi Halfa, in the northern Sudan, MacIver and I had dug a temple and part of the Egyptian town, but, search the desert as we might for two months, we had failed to find any trace of the cemetery which must have been attached to the place. One evening we climbed a little hill behind the house to watch the sunset over the Nile; we were grumbling at our ill luck when suddenly MacIver pointed to the plain at our feet; its whole surface was dotted with dark circles which, though we had tramped over it day after day, we had never seen. I ran down the hill and the circles vanished as I came close to them, but, guided by MacIver from above, I made little piles of gravel here and there, one in the middle of each ring; and when we started digging there next morning our Arab workmen found under each pile the square, rock-cut shaft of a tomb. The original grave-diggers had heaped the splinters of stone round the mouth of the shaft, and when they filled it up again a certain amount remained over; four thousand years had produced a dead level of stone and gravel where the eye could distinguish no difference of arrangement or texture; but for the space of five minutes in the day the sun's rays, coming at a particular angle, brought out a darker tint in the stone which had been quarried from deeper underground—but, even so, the effect could only be seen from above, and perhaps from a single point.

The archæologist, in fact, has to keep his eyes open for evidence of all sorts. At Carchemish, in North Syria, my old Greek foreman, Gregori, an experienced digger if ever there was one, and I, completely mystified our Turkish inspector. We told him we were going to excavate a cemetery, and as we had not previously found graves he was duly interested,

and asked to be shown the spot. We took him
outside the earth ramparts of the old city to a
ploughed field by the river bank, lying fallow
that year, and, pointing to the fragments of
pottery which strewed the ground, explained
that these constituted good evidence for the
existence of a graveyard. Then Gregori and I,
consulting together, started to make piles of
stones marking the position of individual graves.
This was too much for Fuad Beg, who protested
that we were bluffing him; I betted that we
should find a grave under every pile and no
graves at all except where we had put a mark;
he took the bet and lost it, and spent a month
wondering why. It was really a simple case of
deduction. The river bank was of hard gravel,
the made soil overlying it very shallow, and
only disturbed to the depth of about three
inches by the feeble Arab plough; the field,
being fallow, was covered with sparse growth,
for the most part shallow-rooted, but with a
mixture of sturdier weeds of a sort whose roots
go deeply down; if one looked carefully it
became manifest that these weeds were sometimes single, but often in clumps of four or five
plants, but a clump never measured more than
six feet across; at some time or another the
gravel subsoil had been broken up, so that the

plant roots could penetrate it, and it had been broken up in patches which would be just the right size for graves; the broken pottery on the surface represented either shallow burials, or more probably, offerings placed above the graves at ground level, and every deep-growing weed or group of weeds meant a grave-shaft. The deduction proved correct.

In just the same way Professor van Riet Lowe has remarked that in Rhodesia and the Transvaal a quite distinctive flora grows on sites which the ancients used as dumps for rubbish and he tells a story[1] *à propos* of this. At Zimbabwe 'we were standing on the Acropolis and looking down upon the Valley of Ruins I noticed (through my binoculars) an area covered by grass and a particularly unpleasant thorny ground-creeper with masses of small yellow flowers, and indicating this, said "There is a large midden".... When we had descended into the valley we went on to my entirely uninviting patch and judiciously cleared and dug into a few small areas from every one of which we extracted handfuls of potsherds encased in ash'.

The evidence may be something less material

[1] I quote here from O. G. S. Crawford's admirable book *Archæology in the Field*, p. 264.

than grass and weeds. Towards the end of my
first season's work at Atchana in North Syria I
said to my foreman 'Hamoudi, I've always said
that this must be a royal city; we've dug out
some very good private houses, but before we
close down we ought to do a bit of work on the
palace; it would be nice to prove the point'.
Hamoudi concurred heartily. 'You know where
it is, don't you?' I asked. Hamoudi was quite
taken aback; 'Of course I do; don't you?'
'Yes. Just go along and mark out a square that
we can clear in ten days'. He did so, and I
went to look and agreed that he was right on
top of the palace but suggested that as we could
excavate so little of it in the time left to us it
would be best to get part of the façade, and I
shifted his square a few yards to the south-east.
We dug down, and came straight on the front
steps of the royal palace with its columned
portico and entrance-chamber. Now this was
not magic or second sight. We were working
on a long high mound whose axis ran north-
west by south-east; in its heyday it had been a
city enclosed by great walls (this was really the
acropolis, there had probably been a lower
town as well) and the mound's top had been
crowded with close-built houses, and with the
smoke of their charcoal cooking-stoves and

with the very primitive methods of sanitation employed and the heat of the Syrian summer sun the atmosphere must have been, to say the least of it, most unpleasant. The mound rose highest at the north-west end. In the summer the prevailing wind blows from the north-west, from the Anti-Taurus mountains which are capped with snow almost the year round. Obviously the most agreeable site for a house was where you got the benefit of a cool breeze and the wind carried away from you all the smells of the huddled town; that was the site the King was bound to choose: and since the palace needed protection the barracks or castle would be close by where it had too the advantage of commanding the road that ran inland from the sea-coast, and those solid buildings would account for the greater height of the mound at this end. It was a matter of common sense and of human nature, which changes very little; in the plain round Atchana there are mounds still occupied, and invariably the landlord's stone-built house is at the north-west end and the reed or mud huts of his labourers lie to the south-east.

It was deduction of another sort that led to the discovery of Tutankhamen's tomb. The Valley of the Kings at Thebes contained the known graves of all the Pharaohs of the Eighteenth Dynasty except two: clearly it was the burial-ground of the dynasty, therefore *all* the kings of that dynasty ought to have been found there, and since they had not, the missing ones were still to seek, but to seek within the valley confines. For three years the late Lord Carnarvon worked in that part of the valley which was still unexplored, shifting the thousands of tons of limestone chips which filled the bottom of the ravine, scraping the cliff sides in search of a possible doorway, and it was only when the wearisome task was well-nigh done that the astonishing discovery was made: he and Howard Carter owed their success not to a stroke of good luck but to the patient following-out of a logical theory.

Chapter II

The Start of an Excavation

THE AIM OF THE FIELD ARCHÆOLOGIST IS
to discover and to illustrate the course of
human history; that really means that
his task is a complicated one, and the unfortu-
nate man is, in fact, serving two masters whose
interests, though consistent, are not identical.
On the one side he has to get his scientific
record. As I said above, there is more to be
learnt from the facts of discovery than from the
actual things discovered, so that from this
point of view the very finest object, when once
it has yielded up all the historical evidence it
can afford, has exhausted its interest and might
almost as well not exist; thus, if the earthquake
which in 1927 shook Crete had wiped out the
Museum at Candia, with all its contents, instead of merely smashing one or two frescoes, it would have been a great artistic loss,
but scientifically the damage would have been
relatively small, because publication has put on
permanent record the historical results of the

excavations at Knossos, Phaistos and the other
Minoan sites.

On the other hand, the field worker is
generally backed by an institution which is
anxious to acquire specimens for museum
shelves—a perfectly good motive, because an
appeal to the eye is the best way of awakening
interest in a new form of knowledge—'seeing is
believing', and museums are a big factor in
education. The archæologist, therefore, has to
be as careful about the preservation of objects
as about the finding of them, and the demands
on his time are thereby at least doubled. If he
is working in a country like England this does
not so much matter, for he can generally get
in skilled help to deal with an emergency, but
where an expedition has to be self-supporting
one man cannot expect to be able to cope with
all its needs, and there arises the question of the
staff which he is to take with him.

The running of an expedition in the field
involves a great deal beyond the actual dig.
Pay-sheets have to be made out, correspondence
written, accounts kept, the camp has to be
housed and fed: if it is an excavation in which
inscribed documents are found the excavator
must know at least the gist of these, so that he
may keep up to date with his discoveries and

have as much light as possible to direct his course; surveys must be made of the site and plans drawn up of each building as it is found: even assuming that the head of the expedition can do each of these things, he cannot do them all, and so he must provide himself with an architect, and an epigraphist to deal with the inscriptions, and he will require at least one assistant for the general archæological work; four or five people, all specialists in their several lines, are the minimum with which a big excavation can be run successfully. I must emphasize strongly one thing. All excavation is destruction. The archæologist unearths a building, perhaps removing two or three later constructions in order to do so; its walls remain and can be seen or, if the wind-blown sand covers them again, they can be dug out a second time, but all the evidence given by stratification, by the position of objects, by traces of wood ash or by fallen brickwork, has gone, and can never be recovered; he digs out a grave and all that remains is a hole in the ground and a group of objects in a museum; any evidence he has failed to note has gone for ever, and unless his record is scientifically complete he has defrauded science, and would better not have dug at all. With this heavy responsibility he must be assured beforehand that he has a staff sufficient to do full justice to the work he would undertake.

Does the archæologist, then, do no digging himself?

In some sites, especially in a country like England, excavation is often on a very small scale, employing only six or a dozen men, of whom some may be volunteers. interested enough to be very careful and to need less supervision than the casual labourer; in that case the director of the work may well be one of the gang. When excavating a Late Celtic graveyard near Canterbury I could take my turn with pick and barrow and still lose nothing of what my five men were doing; but on a site like Ur work on so small a scale would produce no results at all. There a big gang has to be employed, and because the overhead expenses of travelling and so on are necessarily heavy and the season is short, and because funds for archæological work are hard to raise and must be used to the best advantage, the most economical thing is to engage the largest number of workmen possible, the largest number, that is, that can be profitably employed on the particular site chosen for excavation and with which the staff can adequately cope. This is no fixed figure. If it is proposed to excavate temple ruins, where there is a vast amount of earth to be shifted and objects are likely to be few, a staff of five may manage three hundred men, provided that they have good foremen to back them in the actual supervising. Digging in the great cemetery at Ur, where the graves produced objects in abundance, requiring much fine work and elaborate note-taking, but lay deep down in the soil and so were slow to come at, the same staff was hard put to it to keep pace with a hundred and eighty men; had similar graves been found near the surface our gang would have had to be halved. At Ur the work of a big gang like this is organized as follows. All the men are directly under the orders of three trained and trusted Arab fore-men, who are not Iraqis, but come from far away in North Syria, whereas the workmen are recruited from the neighbourhood. They are divided up into small parties consisting of a pick-man, a spade-man and three or four basket-men; of these the pick-man is selected for his experience and his superior intelligence —he is generally one who has been employed by us for a number of years, and is not so old as to have grown stupid nor too young to exercise authority; he uses an army entrench-

ing-tool (the best tool I know for excavating in
Iraq) and is the head of his little gang; since he
does the actual cutting-away of the soil it is he
who discovers things, and it is up to him to see
that he exposes them without damage. The
second man, armed with a long-handled native
spade, puts the loosened earth into the baskets,
and if the pick-man has missed anything the
spade-man ought to see it: the basket-men are
either the older fools or young recruits, and their
job is purely mechanical—they simply carry
the full baskets to the light railway, tip the
earth into the wagons and come back for more
(*see* Plate IV). As individuals, the basket-men
count, perhaps, for less, but it must be remem-
bered that on the distance which they have to
go and on the pace at which they walk depends
the whole progress—and the cost—of the
excavation; the director has to see to it that
the railhead is as close as possible to the dig, the
foreman that there is no slacking on the road.

The Arab foreman is, next to the archæologist
himself, the most important person on the
excavations, for on him depends the conduct of
the whole gang of diggers. He not only makes
them work—the foreman who sits on the ground
and just yells 'Y'Allah, y'Allah,' is not doing his
job, even though the men run in answer to his

cry; he must be himself the most highly skilled ·
man on the ground, so that he can teach the
rest their business, and take over from them
when anything is likely to overtax their powers
—and that means that he must know the quality
of each individual man, and must carry in his
head exactly what each small gang is doing, so
that he can visualize the difficulty almost before
it arises; he must have that enthusiasm which
inspires the workers to do their best, not merely
because they are driven, but through a pride
in their job; and he must be a diplomatist who
can settle quarrels and keep the gang in a good
temper. Such a man, when found, is a 'jewel
of great price,' and I suppose that there are few
archæologists who do not nurse the belief that
their own particular foreman is the best of his
race.

It is an almost universal rule that the
excavator should pay 'baksheesh' to his men
for the objects they find, over and above their
wages (*see* Plate V). It might be argued that
a workman, paid a fair wage, has no claim to
an extra reward for what his work may produce, but in practice the 'baksheesh' system is
essential. In the first place, the finding of an
object does give you a certain feeling of posses-
sion, and that moral claim warrants compen-

sation if you have to hand the object over to someone else; so the reward is primarily an insurance against theft, and generally it is reckoned at the sum which an agent for an antiquity-dealer might pay for the object were it stolen. Then, it is a direct encouragement to good work; for an object broken by the digger little or no reward is paid, so it is to his interest not only to keep his eyes open but to deal carefully with what he has seen—and where work has been carelessly done it is far less invidious for the archæologist to withhold a reward than to cut from an earned wage. At Ur the gang of five or six men working together is the unit amongst which the 'baksheesh' is distributed; all are paid at a flat rate of wages but the pick-man, who finds most of the things, and has to do the delicate work, gets the lion's share of the reward, the spade-man rather more than half of that, and the basket-men only a small proportion; in every discovery made in their particular patch of ground all have a financial interest, and theft by any one of them would mean the defrauding of the rest, so that mutual suspicion (and the foreman sees to it that the gang is not composed of men likely to league together to steal) practically ensures our losing nothing. Naturally, a pick-

PLATE VII

A Palestinian 'Tell'—Beth Pelet
The excavation starting with the top levels
*(By courtesy of the British School of Archæology in Egypt)*

*(See p. 47)*

PLATE VIII

(a)

(b)

Evidence of date

Temple walls at Ur with royal inscriptions on the bricks
(a) of Bur-Sin, 2220 B.C.
(b) of Kurigalzu, 1400 B.C.

(See p. 52)

man skilled above the average is likely to be put to work where good results may be expected, and therefore does better in 'baksheesh' than the rest; and since the system is extended to giving extra pay for good work as such, even where the finds may have little intrinsic value, all recognize that skill is at a premium, and by degrees they learn to appreciate it for its own sake. On an average season the 'baksheesh' bill may come to fifteen per cent of the wages; it is not very much, but it has an effect which doubling the wages would never produce. The sporting element which it introduces into the unaccustomed routine of work has a special appeal for Arabs, who are gamblers by nature, but I have found it just as effective, I think, with Italian workmen, or English; and the fact that every unexpected stroke of good fortune means luck for them as well as satisfaction to the employer does create an astonishing amount of good will. At al 'Ubaid I had spent three weeks preparing to remove a copper statue of a bull, and at the last moment the whole thing collapsed in useless fragments of green decay; in the dinner-hour I overheard an Arab commiserating with one of the gang concerned on the presumably handsome 'baksheesh' which would have been forthcoming if the operation

4

had succeeded and would now never be paid:
'To hell with the baksheesh,' retorted the other,
and went on to declare that he would gladly
have given a week's pay to have lifted safely
what had cost so much time and trouble. Of
course he would not have surrendered his pay
had it come to the point, but that he could
imagine himself doing so meant that he was
genuinely keen on the success of the work.
Very few men will not take pride in doing a
job well, provided that it gets fair recognition,
and our trained Arabs will take infinite pains
in following up a brick wall, and cleaning the
face of it so as to preserve its mud plaster intact,
even though there is no hope of reward to be
got from it. 'It is in the interest of science!'
they say with resigned cheerfulness, knowing
nothing of what science is; but they do not
disguise their preference for the spot where
objects may await discovery and 'baksheesh'
abound.

The moment a pick-man sees anything of
possible interest, the face of a mud-brick wall,
the green of copper or bronze, a clay pot, or
simply a change in the character of the soil, he
has to report it to the nearest foreman who, taking over the pick, satisfies himself as to what is
really there, and either tells the man to carry

on, giving him the necessary instructions, or calls up one of the staff. Then the archæologist, who the moment before may have been writing notes in a different part of the field, has to take his turn with the pick, or more probably with a knife, and may spend the next few hours crouched in the same hole, in the same uncomfortable attitude, engrossed in the cleaning, recording and safe removal of some one particular fragile object. Obviously the shifting of dirt must be left to the workmen, and such digging as the archæologist has to undertake himself probably involves very little hard manual labour; but, all the same, quite a large proportion of his time *is* spent in digging, and there are few of the really good objects found at Ur which were not excavated wholly or in large part by the hands of the English staff. The difficulty is to combine this necessary work of detail with the supervision and recording of what is going on in all the other parts of the field; every now and then while excavating the cemetery we have had to shift the men temporarily to some other site where, in the upper levels, nothing requiring much supervision was likely to turn up, so that we ourselves might be free to concentrate on the salving of treasures which one or two small gangs had brought to

light.   About that sort of work I shall have
more to say later on; here I have only brought
it in to show how things are organized, and
what is the division of labour; before describing
how objects are dug up I should like to give
some idea of how one starts to find them.

To begin with, there is the choice of a site.
In the early days of archæology this was simple
enough; the great cities of the ancient world
called for excavation and promised rich re-
wards; Athens, Troy, Babylon and Nineveh,
Persian Susa and Egyptian Thebes or Mem-
phis such were bound to produce treasures of
art and history, and in a capital city the best
artists would have been employed and the
scribes would have been kept most busy.   It
is thanks to work done upon these first-class
sites that we now know so much more of the
history and achievements of the old empires
than was known to our greatgrandfathers; not
one of them has been exhausted, has yielded up
all its secrets, but not one has failed to give us
a detailed and a dramatic picture of a centre of
ancient culture.   But every addition to our
knowledge has brought fresh problems, more
far-reaching than the picture we have drawn.
Thus excavations in Italy have illustrated the
entire civilization of the Etruscans; work at

PLATE IX

(a)

(b)

(c)

A 'foundation-deposit' at Ur

(a) The box in the wall foundation
(b) The copper figure of King Rim-Sin (1990 B.C.)
(c) The stone tablet

(See p. 53)

PLATE X

Plaques from the foundation-deposit of a Nubian King
(*By courtesy of the Trustees, The British Museum*)

(*See p. 53*)

Mycenæ and at Tiryns has shown us the glorious state of the Achæan kings of whom Homer sang; but who the Etruscans and the Achæans were and whence they came we have not found out, and no digging in Italy or Greece is likely to tell us; for the sources of a familiar civilization we may have to search far afield. And since we need an answer to such problems if we are to understand the old world as a whole, the wise archæologist, planning a dig, will not let himself be spell-bound by a famous name. He will pass the outstanding questions in review and try to think where the solution of any one of them is most likely to be found, taking into account history and legend, geography, language and what he knows already about different cultures, and so he may be led to some district—a wide district perhaps —within which he must select the actual spot that seems to offer the best promise.

Supposing that an excavator, having done all this, has taken the field, has pitched his camp and has enrolled his men, and proposes to begin work on the site of some buried town where no digging has been done before and there is no previous knowledge to guide him, what is his first step to be?

First of all he will study surface indications.

The site may be large, and he must choose a
particular point of attack; very likely there
may be something visible which may influence
his choice.  In Egypt the town mounds may
cover many acres, but the position of a temple
may be betrayed by fragments of stone, con-
spicuous where most buildings would have been
of mud brick, or by patches of white dust,
showing where a later generation has pulled
out the buried stones and burnt them for lime.
Where stone has been the usual building
material the poorer houses would have walls of
unshaped rubble only, and the presence of cut
blocks holds out promise of something better. In
Syria and Palestine a single isolated mound or
*tell* generally represents the ancient city, and
here its shape may give some inkling of what
lies beneath—the higher lump at one end of a
long ridge may be the fort or palace whose
more solid walls have produced a greater mass
of debris; a ring-mound broken by a gap at one
point will stand for the ramparts and the town
gate. In Mesopotamia, where a tangle of linked
mounds may stretch for miles, the highest may
be buildings deliberately raised on artificial
platforms, such as the Ziggurat, or, in the
majority of cases, they denote the quarters
where human occupation has been most con-

tinuous, and the height is due to the repeated building of new houses over the ruins of the old. Very often the question can be solved by the broken pottery lying on the mound's surface. Thus at Warka or Erech, a very extensive site, one mound was obviously the Ziggurat or staged tower; another, littered with sherds of Parthian pottery, showed that its upper levels belonged to the very latest date at which the town had been inhabited; on the other hand a low bank on which one could pick up fragments of painted pottery and chips of flint or obsidian clearly represented part of the earliest settlement which either had never been built over in later times or, if it were, had been so denuded by wind and water that only the most primitive strata remained; on yet another mound quantities of Kassite potsherds, unmixed with any' of later date, showed that building on that particular spot ceased soon after 1000 B.C. Provided, then, that he can date his pottery, the archæologist has something to guide his choice, but in any case, whether he choose blindly or with reason, his method of action will probably be the same whatever his point of attack; he will begin by trenching.

A line is marked either right across a mound or from the top of it to well beyond its foot, and along this the gangs are placed with a measured square for each to work in; before the trench has got very deep, there are sure to appear fragments of walls running across it. Now the first point to settle is, whether these disconnected bits of walling are of the same date; if they are not, and in the case of a fairly high and steep mound they are pretty sure not to be, then one has to select the latest and concentrate on them; for to dig out simultaneously two buildings of different dates is to ask for trouble; it will become difficult, if not impossible, to assign objects to their right levels, and failing to get things in their true context we shall lose or confuse the chronological evidence, which is the main aim of archæology. For the same reason trench-work ought to be stopped as soon as it has served its purpose by finding out the whereabouts of buildings, and the men should be switched off to follow the walls to right and left; it is wisest to work from the known to the unknown, and a wall is a good solid fact. In Egypt the task is generally an easy one, for Egyptian ruins are covered by sand and the sand falls readily away from the walls of mud brick or, more often, of hewn stone. It is far more difficult in moister soil to excavate mud brick buildings buried in the ruin of their own walls, for then the wall is of the same nature as the rubbish which lies against it, and it requires skill to distinguish between fallen and standing brickwork. I have known an archæologist in Egypt, digging for the first time on a site of this sort, cut away every brick wall he encountered until, of a building which when he started was standing six feet high, there was left nothing but the thresholds of the doors, which happened to be of stone. Even stone walls are not always easy to follow; if built of rough rubble with mud for mortar they may have no true face left; the mortar may have oozed out, the stones slipped, until there is little to choose between the wall and the fallen rubble heaped against it; in the case of a wall faced with properly cut blocks, the face may have been carried off by a later generation as material for another building and there may remain only a rubble core which scarcely looks like masonry at all. The greatest test of an excavator's skill in this branch of his work is when he has to deal with *terre pisée*, walls built not of bricks but of mere mud rammed together—a primitive substitute for reinforced concrete. Here there is no clean-cut face to guide him, little difference of texture to distinguish wall from heaped rubbish, and he has to work almost as much by faith as by sight;

if, days later, when drying brings out the nuances of colour, he can assure himself that he has neither cut into his walls nor made false walls by leaving what is mere earth standing in the semblance of building, he will have good reason to feel pleased with himself.

Even with good mud brick the work is not always easy. At Warka (the ancient Erech) in Mesopotamia the top of the Ziggurat mound seemed to yield nothing but a uniform and level mass of mud brickwork. The wind cleared away the dust from its surface and the German excavators noticed here and there straight white lines, no wider than the thickness of a sheet of notepaper, and following these up they discovered the ground-plan of a building; it was a temple whose rooms had been neatly filled with brickwork so as to make a raised platform for a later structure, but the original walls had been whitewashed and when they were trimmed down the section of that thin coating distinguished the brickwork of the walls from that of the filling; but it required the eye of faith to see it. Similarly on a temple site at Atchana in North Syria where again rooms had been filled with well-laid bricks to make a platform but there was no whitewash to guide us, we found that if we scraped the surface of what seemed to be a featureless mass in the morning, after the night dews had moistened the brick, and then left it for a while, the ground-plan would appear, because the walls, with their deeper foundations, held the moisture longer and would still be dark in colour when the filling had dried to a lighter tint; but ten minutes later the ground-plan would fade away and uniform brickwork again confront the sun.

The finding of walls then may be easy or may be difficult, but it is the essential preliminary; only when there is something definite to go upon can the excavation follow rational lines.

While one gang goes ahead along each face of each wall, cutting a narrow trench for the purpose, others behind them go deeper to find floors if possible, and the rest are set to clear the rooms as these appear. If there be a distinguishable floor, whether of brick or of beaten earth, well and good, that should be for the moment the depth-limit of the excavation; and if there be none, the work should stop short where the floor ought to be, that is, a little above the level to which the wall foundations go down. The sense of this is clear. Everything found above floor level is contemporary with or later than the building, everything found below the floor is earlier (*see* Plate VI); the man who stamped down that mud to make a pavement for his house was sealing up an archæological stratum, and it behoves us to profit by his good work, and not to confuse the evidence which he has made so clear. Therefore, the top building must be cleared first, its plan drawn out, its contents duly noted, especially the types of pottery found in it, and then, when everything that can be learnt about it and from it has been learnt, it must all be swept away, its foundations rooted out, and the excavation of the next level can begin.

In practice this is not always as simple as it may sound. Sometimes a house has been ruined and buried, but parts of its walls have been left sticking up above ground, and the next builder on the site has incorporated them in his new house, so that the same walls really belong to two different periods. One house may have stood unchanged while its neighbour was rebuilt twice over, so that what is found in the rooms of the first corresponds in date to the contents of three distinct floor levels next door; or again, neighbouring houses of exactly the same date may, thanks to some accident of past building, stand at very different levels. All sorts of things such as these may confuse the issues, and it is the duty of the archæologist to

PLATE XI

The Palace of Minos at Knossos      *(See p. 57)*

Reconstructed drawing of part of the West Palace wing facing on the central court

*(By permission of Sir Arthur Evans)*

PLATE XII

(a)

(b)

The Palace of Minos at Knossos: Restoration of the actual building
(a) Room of the Priest-King
(b) Stepped porch and central staircase
(By permission of Sir Arthur Evans)

(See p. 56)

detect and make proper allowances for them, which he could never succeed in doing if he were not strict in his method and if that method were not controlled by common-sense. We habitually speak of 'archæological levels' and, describing our excavations, refer an object to 'Level VI' or 'Level IV' as evidence for its date; that implies careful measurement. But what is an 'archæological level'? Sometimes a digger, determined to be on the right side, has started with a fixed datum line, such as the highest point on the surface of his site, and recorded the exact depth below that line at which every object was found—then the first ten inches, let us say, make up Level I, the next ten inches Level II, and so on; and this schematized section of the soil becomes his basis for chronology. There are occasions where the method is necessary and valuable, as, for instance, in making a section of a trench in an ancient earth-work; but for a town site it is worse than useless. Not only does it fail to take into account those accidents of building which I have just mentioned, but in the Middle East, at any rate, where town sites have resulted in the gradual formation of a *tell* or mound, the houses were necessarily stepped down the mound's sides so that those on the outskirts may

be twenty feet or more below those in the
centre; a horizontal line drawn through the
middle of the mound fifteen feet below the
top-surface datum-line so far from giving a
single archæological level might cut through
half a dozen levels of which that in the middle
would be centuries older than that on the
circumference. Pure mathematics must here
be controlled by observation and common
sense, and the archæological 'level' must
correspond to historical fact.

To the general rule that one should begin at
the top and go down layer by layer, there is one
exception, justified only when the prime object
of the work is not to clear buildings but to
obtain certain definite information. It may be
essential to find out from the outset the character of a mound, whether it represents a long
period or a single phase of history, and by
digging from the top we shall learn that only
by slow degrees; or our knowledge of the
archæology of a country may be so slight that
we shall have difficulty in assigning what we
find in the successive levels to the right points
in the time-sequence—we need a rule with
which to measure our discoveries. Then a
different method can be employed.

In Palestine a certain amount of scrappy

digging had been done, but no connected
history had been traced, and in particular very
little had been learnt about the pottery, and
the changing types of pottery vessels are the
best criterion of date that an archæologist can
have. In 1891 Flinders Petrie went to dig at
Lachish, in south Palestine, an old Biblical city
now represented by a mound whose earth sides
rose steeply from the plain, and he simply drove
a trench into the steep side from top to bottom
(*see* Plate VII).

His pick-men, set one above the other at fixed distances up the slope, had each to cut into
it a horizontal step; the objects, broken pottery
and so on, found by each gang were kept apart
and recorded separately. The division by
gangs, was, of course, artificial, not answering
to anything in the stratification of the mound,
but when the notes on each level were complete, and could be compared, the scientific
results were perfectly clear. The types of
pottery varied with the altitude; a shape
common in the topmost five feet of soil might be
rare in the next five, and entirely absent in the
next; one could therefore put its starting-point
at seven or eight feet from the summit of the
mound and assume that it continued in fashion
as long as the town was inhabited. A type

might be found in fair quantities by one pick-man in his horizontal shaft and not by either of the men above and below him; confined to a narrow stratum, it must have been a short-lived type, and so the more valuable for dating because it allowed a smaller margin of error. There was no evidence for fixing exact dates because there were no written documents; but in a very short time Petrie was able to work out a schematic chart, in which every type of vessel found by him was assigned to its proper place in a historical sequence; for the first time Palestinian archæology was provided with a sound chronological basis.

It might be thought that this was the natural result of a very simple process, but actually there are few things more difficult than the working-out of a step-trench cut in the side of the mound. Petrie succeeded because he was an archæological genius, but others have been less fortunate. I remember visiting the excavation of a lofty *tell* in India. On the very top they had cleared house ruins which were dated by coins and pottery to the Kushan period, and from the edge of the house site a deep cut had been made, with two or three steps, into the steep side of the mound, and here, just twenty-six feet below the houses, they had found groups

PLATE XIII

Palace of Minos at Knossos: Reconstruction of the actual remains

(*By permission of Sir Arthur Evans*)

(*See p.* 56)

PLATE XIV

SECTION A·B

(a)

(b)

A temple at el-Amarna

(a) The ground plan as found
(b) The ground plan as restored
(c) Suggested restoration of Group II
    on Section A.B

(*By courtesy of the Egyptian Exploration Society*)

(*See pp.* 59–61)

(c)

of pottery and coins of precisely the same date as those on the house floors! The facts were indisputable, and they seemed to make nonsense of any time sequence; the excavators were at their wit's end. What had happened was that the workmen, digging in horizontally from the slope of the mound, had failed to notice (as they would almost inevitably fail) the slight difference in soil that marked the filling of ancient rubbish-pits which ran down into the ground from house-level; when therefore they came on the pots lying at the bottom there was nothing to connect them with the upper surface —or, at least, nothing very obvious. If the pits had contained pottery only one would have argued that the Kushan potters were very conservative and produced the same models for several centuries; but the presence of coins forced one to look for another explanation, and actually it was in one case possible to see, in the face of the cut soil, the two faint grey lines of discoloured earth that marked the sides of the rubbish-pit descending from house level to the cluster of pots at its bottom. The archæologist's task is indeed beset with pitfalls.

## Chapter III

## Work on a Town Site

DIGGING ON OUR TOWN SITE BEGAN WITH a single long trench.. Very soon this changed its appearance and spread to right and left, first with narrow trenches, then with rectangular clearings like so many shallow boxes separated by low walls. Now the ruins so long buried begin to take on shape and meaning, and the archæologist is faced with fresh problems.

The first thing he will want to do is to establish the date and character of the building. Very often the date can be fixed only by the objects found between the walls, and then the exactness of the date will depend on how much is known of the antiquities, and particularly of the pottery, of the country. A Roman site in Britain can usually be brought within fairly narrow limits; even if no coins are found—and they are generally forthcoming—the local pottery is being studied with more and more definite results, and the red *terra sigillata* wares

imported from the south of Gaul and from the
Rhine factories give very accurate information,
for we know within a few years when some of
the potters were at work. In classical Greece
the household wares are not properly classified,
but even a fragment of a red- or black-figured
vase can nearly always be dated to within
thirty years, and though such precision is
impossible in the pre-classical age and we have
to be content with periods, these are being
more closely defined, and when we can describe
a house as 'Middle Minoan III' we are really
saying all that it is essential to know. An exact
chronology is of course the archæologist's aim,
but this can only be obtained by combining the
results of many excavations and making use
of such dateable objects as they may have
produced. And the measure of success achieved
is gratifying. When I wrote this book, in 1930,
I was obliged to say that in Palestine and Syria
the terms employed were even vaguer than
those for the Greek world; the local pottery
could still only be grouped into classes, such as
'Late Bronze Age', 'Early Iron Age', each of
which covered several centuries; 'but even so',
I added, 'we have a foundation on which the
steps of a historic sequence can be built up'.
Well, it has now been built. We now have a

Middle Bronze Age divided into four sub-periods, a Late Bronze Age also of four sub-periods, giving, between the twentieth and the twelfth centuries, an average length for each sub-period of only a hundred years; and the Iron Age, from 1200 B.C. to 330 B.C., is divided into three phases.[1] This remarkable advance was made possible by the occurrence in Palestine and Syria of dateable Egyptian imports associated with local objects whose place in the sequence could be fixed on purely archæological grounds.

In Mesopotamia a temple will often have in its walls a certain number of bricks on which there has been written or stamped an inscription giving the name of the temple, of the god to whom it was dedicated, and of the king by whose order or in whose honour it was put up (*see* Plate VIII); here the archæologist is given all the information he can expect. It may be that at different heights in the walls, or at different places, he may find brick inscriptions of different kings; this means that a later ruler has repaired the building of his predecessor, and with each name a new chapter can be added to the temple's history. Mesopotamian

[1] On this see Professor Albright's 'Pelican' book *The Archæology of Palestine.*

kings were very fond of recording their piety as
temple-builders, and the inscription may appear
not only on the bricks of the structure but also
on clay cones hidden in the core of the wall, on
the great stones which were set in brick boxes
below floor level in the doorways to act as
hinges for the doors, or again on copper figures
and stone tablets (*see* Plate IX) which were
placed as 'foundation-deposits' under the walls,
just as to-day we may bury in a similar box
coins of the realm and copies of newspapers. In
Egyptian temples there will be inscriptions on
the walls, and under the corner-stones foundation-deposits with the king's name inscribed
on tablets of gold, silver, copper, stone, and
wood, all the materials used in the construction
of the building (*see* Plate X). Or there may be
evidence of other kinds. At Carchemish, the
Hittites, the Greeks and the Romans worked
different quarries, and the quality of the stone in
the walls served as a rough guide to dating until
better evidence turned up. In Mesopotamia
the shape and size of bricks varied fairly con-
sistently at different periods, and by recording
the dimensions of bricks whose age is fixed by
inscriptions one obtains a tolerably reliable
criterion for fixing the period of private houses
and other buildings in which no inscribed bricks

occur—in fact, after a time a mere glance enables one to make a pretty good guess at a wall's date. Absolute precision is too much to be hoped for—though recently at Ur an inscription did give us the actual year in which the temple we were excavating was founded— but in nearly every case the archæologist ought to be able, by evidence of one kind or another, to define within reasonable limits the age of any buildings he digs up.

Then for the character of the building. An inscription may give the *fact* that it was a temple, but what we really want to know is, what kind of a temple or what kind of a house was it? Here comes in the importance of the plan. I remember hearing an antiquary of the old school declare that to dig out a ruin for the sake of its plan was a waste of money, because nobody understood or cared about plans—at any rate he didn't. Well, the business of the archæologist is precisely to understand plans; he may have a professional architect to help him in the field work, but he must be something of an architect himself, and he will have just as much to do with the building on paper as with the scraps of brick or stone walling from which the paper plan is drawn up. The ground plan sums up what he has found of his building, and is the basis of what he will find out about it. One need not ask the layman to be enthusiastic about the plan of an ancient building, but the professional should, with the help of the plan, get information about the building which the layman will find of interest. We are digging up the past—not the existing ruin, but the temple or house which it once was; the ground-plan is the first and most obvious thing that we secure, but on it we have to build up by the help of all the evidence we can find, and all the knowledge we possess, the original edifice; that cannot always be done, but until it is done the archæologist has not fully succeeded; and with this aim in view he must observe and record and weigh each fact, however minute and seemingly unimportant, that may help his task.

First of all, he has to decide what the plan is. Some walls may have been destroyed altogether and their line be but conjectural, though every effort must be made to support conjecture by evidence; I have known a Roman wall in Britain to be accurately planned when it had altogether ceased to exist. The Roman builder dug a trench for his foundations and put in it a bedding of clay for his stonework; here every stone had vanished, but a film of clay was traced for many yards through the loam of the meadow and gave the outline of the building. Or the walls may be too many, a senseless confusion, some being due to additions to or alterations of the original structure, and on paper these, which have their historical value all right, will have to be eliminated before the first builder's intentions become clear. And his main intention will be clear at once. Seldom could one mistake the ground-plan of a temple for that of a private house or of a fort. Passages, doorways and rooms give the general arrangement, questions of lighting may show that one 'room' was necessarily an open courtyard; the thickness of walls may give a hint as to the existence of upper storeys; the bases of columns may be found, and a known canon of proportions between the length of a column and its diameter will show the building's height; a shaped stone or a specially moulded brick found loose in the ruins may prove the existence of arched doorways or vaulted roofs. In Crete, Sir Arthur Evans has actually rebuilt up to the second floor part of the Palace of Minos (*see* Plates XII and XIII), though the walls he found were standing only a few courses of stone high; basing his work partly on logical deductions from the plan, partly on minute observation of what was found in the course of the digging—the exact height and position of a threshold stone high up in the soil, the impression left in the earth by a wooden column whose substance had long since vanished, he has been able to bring before the eyes of the ordinary man (who certainly would not have cared for ground-plans!) the actual setting in which the Minoan kings lived their splendid lives (*see* Plate XI). Let me, at the risk of egoism, give an extreme example of what a ground-plan may do in the way of reconstruction.

We were digging at Tell el-Amarna, in Egypt, the site of the city built by Akhenaton, the 'heretic king' who in the fourteenth century before Christ tried to impose a monotheistic religion on a people whose gods were legion. We visited a spot at the south end of the city where, inside a great walled enclosure, the sand, over a fairly large square area, was littered with fragments of worked stone. There were two battered column drums, one or two moderately-sized building stones with carving in relief on two faces, but nearly all the rest were scraps and splinters from carved blocks which had been hopelessly broken up; it was clear that the heretic temple had later been used as a quarry, its walls pulled down, their ornament defaced and the material carried off to be employed elsewhere. It did not look a promising site, but I decided to excavate it on the chance that something worth having might have been left. Results were speedily forthcoming, and nothing could have been more disappointing than they seemed. Everything was on the surface; six inches down, immediately beneath the stone-masons' chippings, there extended a flat rectangular bed of cement, a foot or so thick, laid down over the unstable desert sand as a foundation for the temple; there could be nothing underneath it, all that was above it we had seen before we began to dig. Of the temple not a single stone remained in position, scarcely a stone remained on the site.

On the cement foundation the limestone blocks for wall and floor had been bedded in mortar; when they were pulled up for removal it generally happened that the mortar was left adhering to the cement and bore on its upper surface the impression of the stone; we could count the stones which were not there, and even see the toolmarks on them; looking at them carefully I thought it might be possible to distinguish between the blocks which had been set in lines for the walls and those which had been the pavement of the rooms, so I told the workmen to sweep the whole surface clean with brooms. As Mr. Newton, the architect of the party, and myself were examining the site, trying to decide whether it was worth while making a plan of the position of the blocks, we saw a peculiar thing.

Sometimes the mortar had come away with the stone, leaving the face of the cement clean, and here and there on the clean face there were faint red marks which carried on the lines of the mortar-impressions of what we supposed to be wall blocks. The explanation was obvious. When the cement foundation was dry the builders had worked out on it the architect's plan; a cord dipped in red paint had been stretched taut along the line of each proposed wall, the middle of it lifted and allowed to come slap down again on the cement with the result that a red streak was left as straight as if ruled with a ruler; between two such lines the builder laid his wall-stones. We had no need to exercise our imagination, we had before us the actual plan drawn out by the Egyptian architect (*see* Plate XIV [a]). Having transferred this to paper we could proceed to the next part of our task—to find out what the building was really like. The thickness of the walls varied considerably; a good many of the stone fragments bore reliefs on both sides and therefore must have gone right through from one face of a wall to the other, and they were not all of the same length. All such fragments were collected and measured, and assigned to one or other of the walls shown on the plan according as their length agreed with the wall's thickness.

Now the temple sculptors of Akhenaton's day had a very limited stock of subjects, and the scenes carved on the temple walls repeat each other monotonously; although we had only a few little scraps to represent each wall face, by identifying the subject and looking up parallels to it in better-preserved buildings it was easy to complete on paper the entire decoration of every wall. Two stone drums from columns of different sizes and types lay on the surface, and the plan showed that columns of two sizes had been employed; we would put our drums in their places and, since the proportions of Egyptian columns are pretty consistent, could decide their length, and therefore the height of the building. A few fragments of cornice took us up to the roof-line, a carved lintel completed the main door; we were able to restore accurately and in every

detail (*see* Plate XIV [c]) a temple (incidentally a temple of a new type and therefore a
valuable document for the history of Egyptian
architecture) of which not one stone remained
in position, and all but two or three had been
smashed to atoms. One little detail gave us
perhaps the greatest satisfaction of all. The
flat cement foundation was considerably larger
than the area of the building, and all round it,
outside the walls, there were round holes about
six inches across driven through the cement
while it was still soft into the desert sand beneath; these puzzled us for a while, then, search-
ing carefully, I found in one traces of decayed
wood and the mystery was solved. In the pictures we have of Egyptian temples there are
always shown alongside them flagstaffs from
which pennants were flown; here—and it is the
only case in all Egypt where evidence of the
sort has survived—we had the actual sockets for
the flagstaffs, and in our drawing even that
detail could be put in with measured accuracy.

I have described elsewhere the process of
observation and deduction by which we were
able to work out the original appearance of a
private house at Ur in the time of Abraham.
That is a case where, I think, everyone feels
the genuine interest of the result, because it

supplies a new and unexpected background to
a familiar figure, and challenges us to re-cast
our judgment of him; it is a very obvious case,
because we had been accustomed to think of
Abraham as a simple dweller in tents, and find
him a possible occupant of a sophisticated brick
house in a city; but there was more to it than
that. A building style is neither an accident
nor an arbitrary thing, but a natural growth
answering to the conditions of life; an ancient
building therefore is important, not merely as
illustrating the history of architecture but as a
setting for the lives of men and women, and as
one of their chief forms of self-expression; if we
do not know in what surroundings people
moved and had their being we shall understand very little of their attitude towards life.
To a large extent the influence of the building
on the man is, of course, intangible; in so far
as it crystallizes past traditions it is very real,
but it is not directly translated into bricks and
mortar. We can feel sure that the occupant of
one of the Ur houses did inherit the spirit
which had informed and grown out of centuries
of splendid achievement in civilization and art,
but we deduce that not from the mere existence
of arched doorways and galleried courtyards
but from the fact that such come in unbroken

descent from the royal tombs of fifteen hundred years before. The 'background' so essential to our understanding is something much more than the individual house; but it is none the less true that the actual ruins may give us, together with the architectural reconstruction, some particular feature which we can translate in terms of human thought.

By the time we had excavated a number of the private houses of Abraham's date it was clear that though no two were the same, yet there was a common idea underlying all of them; all were modifications of one general plan, and, therefore, each helped to explain the others. We could compare them and so identify the individual rooms in each; this was the kitchen, this the reception-room, this the lavatory, and so on; experience had taught the ancient architect exactly what type of house suited the habits of the people and the climate of southern Mesopotamia, and so well had he learnt his lesson that he set a standard for all time, and the modern Arab house of Baghdad is but a replica of that in which Abraham might have lived. So one could argue backwards too, and use one's knowledge of the present-day Arab to explain the way of life of the inhabitant of the same land three or four thousand years

ago. And there was more than this. At the
back of virtually every house there was a rather
long and narrow courtyard which always presented the same features;—one end had been
open to the sky and under its paved floor there
was a burial vault (*see* Plate XV), while at the
other end, below a pent-house roof, the pavement was raised and on it stood a low brick
bench or table, a square brick altar in the corner, and in the back wall a fireplace for burning
incense; when we could show that the ordinary
householder of the time had in his house a
special chapel set apart for domestic worship
and that his forebears were buried there so that
they too could take part in the family rites, then
we had really learnt something about him,
about his beliefs and thoughts, which, as a
matter of fact, literature did not tell us and we
should never have guessed.

Sometimes the picture of past life that a
building gives is extraordinarily vivid. At
el-Amarna we dug out a model village (*see*
Plate XVI) put up for the labourers who excavated the rock-cut tombs made in the desert
hills for the aristocracy of the capital; it had
been built all on one plan, and had been de-
serted when the court of Egypt moved back
again to Thebes and no more tomb-making

PLATE XV

A private chapel in a house at Ur showing the altar, the raised pavement of the chancel, and in the foreground the burial vault below the floor

(*See p.* 64)

PLATE XVI

Plan of the 'model village' for workmen at el-Amarná

(*By courtesy of the Egyptian Exploration Society*)

(*See p.* 64)

was required. A square walled enclosure was entirely filled with rows of small houses divided by narrow streets; except for the foreman's quarters near the gate they were all monotonously alike, each with its kitchen-parlour in front (*see* Plate XVII), its bedrooms and cupboard behind, the very pattern of mechanically devised industrial dwellings. That alone was an interesting sidelight on the social conditions of the fourteenth century before Christ in Egypt, and supplemented well the information that the site of the capital itself gave us as to the palaces of the Government officials and the houses of the middle class. But it was the details which made the thing live. Against one front door was a manger built up of mud and stone; in the side of it was contrived a square hole, across which was fixed a stick, and tied round this and trailing across the street was still the palm-fibre rope with which the donkey had been made fast more than three thousand years before. Inside the houses rough paintings on the mud walls hinted at the efforts of the individual workman to improve his surroundings or to express his piety; the charms and amulets picked up on the floor showed which of all the many gods of Egypt were most in favour with working men; scattered tools

6

and implements told of the work of each, or of his pursuits in leisure hours. One house seemed to betray in really comic fashion the character of its owner. Whereas all its neighbours in the row opened on the street running to the east, this was the reverse way round, and opened on a back lane whose boundary was otherwise a blank wall. So striking an exception made us look more closely at the structure, and we found that the house as first built had been like all the rest, giving on the eastern street, but at some time or other it had been remodelled; the front parlour had been divided up into bed-rooms, the old bedrooms thrown into a single room, and through its back wall a new front doorway cut. One could picture the owner who had quarrelled with his neighbours and hated the very sight of them, yet could not leave his house without running into one or another; being little better than a serf tied to his work, he could not move elsewhere to avoid their company; at last, in desperation, he changed not the position but the direction of his home, walled up the front door and made a new one at the back, and one can imagine the relief with which he made his escape into the empty lane, where there was no risk of meeting his enemies.

It might be objected that this is a chronicle of very small beer, and so it is; of course it does not matter one bit whether a few workmen lived on bad terms with each other thirty-three centuries ago; but that is not the point. The point is that ruins may preserve the record even of such trifles as this, supposing that one can read the evidence; if the archæologist is duly careful in observing and recording his observations he may be rewarded with facts of history far more important. It is his business to find out not only what was the building he digs up and what it looked like before it was buried, but through what vicissitudes it passed, for these may reflect the fortunes of a family or even of a nation. Suppose that a thousand years from now the history of England was forgotten, London a buried ruin, and some lucky excavator chanced on the site of Westminster Abbey; with what remained of its structure and its monuments he could re-write whole chapters of the past and recall half of the great names and great events of English history. The archæologist cannot hope for such good fortune as that, but from the ruins of quite an ordinary building he may learn a great deal the interest of which extends beyond the mere fabric which he has discovered; he can link up the dumb witness of bricks and mortar and the odds and ends of jetsam with the life of the people. This is so essential a part of the archæologist's task that an instance of its working may well be given at length.

The temple of the Moon goddess at Ur was originally built in mud brick by Bur-Sin, king of Ur, about 2100 B.C.; a century later it was rebuilt in burnt brick; some time afterwards it was destroyed by fire. That is the barest statement of the facts.

Bur-Sin's building was extremely solid, and might have lasted very much longer than it did; that it so soon had to be restored from floor level upwards must have been due to its destruction by the Elamites, who brought Bur-Sin's dynasty to an end, and sacked the city of Ur. The new walls contain burnt bricks stamped with the inscription of the second founder; this was Enannatum, a priestess, the daughter of the last king of Isin. After the Elamite invasion the overlordship of Mesopotamia passed from Ur to a line of kings who made the city of Isin the capital of the country, and Ur ranked as subject to them; it was favoured, in that the king's daughter took office as priestess there, and it was rich, insomuch that the ruined temple could be rebuilt

PLATE XVII

(See p. 65)

The 'parlour' of a workman's house at el-Amarna

*(By courtesy of the Egyptian Exploration Society)*

PLATE XVIII

(a) Cylinder seals from Egypt, early dynastic period
(*British Museum*)

(b) Impressions of early cylinder seals from Mesopotamia

(*See p.* 74)

on more costly lines than in the old days; we
may conclude that Ur was passing through a
phase of prosperous mediocrity. But Enannatum dedicates her building 'for the life' not
of her royal father but of the king of another
city, Larsa, who was her father's rival, and
eventually wrested from him the overlordship
of the country, founding a new dynasty of
Mesopotamian kings. If the priestess thus
shifts her loyalty while still boasting of her
royal birth, we must suppose that the ascen-
dancy of Larsa over Isin was gained by slow
and more or less peaceful means; certainly it
implies that Ur submitted with a good grace
to the change of masters and continued in com-
fort. In the ruins there were found scattered
clay tablets whose written dates mentioned
virtually all the kings of Larsa in succession—
business documents which spoke of a quiet life.
But in the courtyard, on and around a solid
base of brickwork, there was a litter of chips of
black stone, fragments of a large monument
bearing an inscription in two languages, the
Sumerian tongue of the south country and the
Semitic speech of Babylon and the north; it
had been a monument set up by and recording
the exploits of Hammurabi, the great conqueror
and lawgiver (identical, as we believe, with that

Amraphel whose raiders Abraham defeated by the Dead Sea). Hammurabi conquered Larsa and won for Babylon the suzerainty of the whole land; Ur submitted, and in this temple the victor set up his war memorial. It had been broken to atoms. Inside the temple the brick pavement was covered with a thick layer of charred wood and ashes; mixed with these were hundreds of fragments of stone vases, some of them bearing the dedications of kings already ancient in Hammurabi's time, broken statues and more tablets from the temple archives; the temple had been sacked as well as burnt. The dates on the new series of tablets took us down through Hammurabi's reign, and up to the eleventh year of the reign of his son, and then they stopped short. Now the eleventh year was called 'that in which the south country rebelled' and the twelfth year 'that in which the King destroyed the walls of Ur.' Those two phrases tell us all that we knew of contemporary history; now put them side by side with the archæological evidence and the story is plain. Ur had submitted quietly to Hammurabi, but joined in, if it did not lead, the rebellion against his son, and its citizens signalized their revolt by defacing the war-memorial of Babylon. Within a few months, before the litter of stone which symbolized independence had been cleared away from the Moon goddess' court, the northern troops had stormed the walls of Ur and, not content with dismantling its defences, had sacked its shrines, breaking into the treasuries and looting the precious metal, while they smashed on the pavements what was not worth carrying away, and had finished by setting fire to the temple and to all the quarter in which it stood. Not only could we win from the ruins a detailed and a dated account of the buildings' foundation and destruction, but we could see in it an epitome of the town's history over the space of three hundred years.

I have chosen this instance chiefly because here the main facts were already known; the archæological results of the dig had to be worked out independently, and then brought into relation with the records, and you can see how at every point they could be checked by external evidence and proved correct. Very often there is no previously recorded history, and the archæologist is thrown back on his own resources; his deductions will not necessarily be beyond dispute, but I hope that I have shown that if they are logically based on the evidence they have every chance of being good history.

Suppose that he is digging into a mound where the remains of buildings lie one above the other in more or less definite strata, but all belong to a period or to a culture of which there is no written record; what sort of evidence is he going to find? That there should be material to illustrate the life of a forgotten people we may grant, but how can he arrive at historical events? at the sort of things that ancient chronicles might have told us?

Here comparative archæology must come into play. Suppose that his lowest strata belong to the neolithic age, and yield little in the way of objects other than stone implements and shreds of rough, hand-made pottery; even so there are probably affinities with other sites, and he can decide to what branch of culture the earliest inhabitants must be assigned.

As the levels rise stone will give place to metal. It may be that the copper tools and weapons appear quite suddenly in a certain stratum, yet in forms that seem well established, the work not of a beginner but of a craftsman experienced in the use of metal; we look elsewhere and in some other country find the same forms of weapons and tools, but there their evolution can be traced from something simpler, perhaps from stone originals; then it is manifest that on our site they are not local products but imports from abroad. Perhaps while the revolutionary change from stone to metal takes place the pottery shows a perfectly uniform development; pottery-making is essentially a local industry, and if that is unaffected we can argue that the population did not change, and that the introduction of metal was due to peaceful penetration or trade. But suppose the excavator comes upon a 'burnt stratum.' A patch of ashes may result from mere accident and mean nothing; ashes spread over the greater part of a site and accompanied with the marks of burning on walls tells of the destruction of the town. Suppose now that in the stratum above the ashes there appear new forms of pottery having no kinship with what has gone before; this implies foreign influence, and, taken in conjunction with the evidence of destruction, points to foreign conquest, and if the new pottery can be traced the identity of the conquerors can be established. Instead of the ashes of a fire there may be a layer of wind-blown sand, or a bed of mud finely stratified as successive rain-storms have brought down dust and decaying brick to fill up the hollows where the water lay; these tell of the desertion of a site, and may introduce a change of inhabitants.

In the *tells*, or mounds, of southern Palestine, the early Bronze Age settlements with their rough walls and native pottery give place to strata where more solid walls and new types of weapons, glazed scarabs and beads mark the Egyptian conquest of Syria. Higher up again the sudden appearance of iron weapons and of a very distinctive painted pottery unlike anything known in the country before, but closely akin to wares found in Asia Minor, bears witness to the invasion of the Philistines; we think of Goliath, with his iron armour, and of the Chalybes whom Homer had heard tell of as an Asia Minor race, who got their name as being the first workers in iron.

Sometimes the link is there but its meaning has to be argued out. In Egypt at the time of the First Dynasty, about 3150 B.C., we find cylinder seals used, little engraved stone or shell cylinders which were rolled on clay to make the sign-manual of the owner (*see* Plate XVIII); precisely similar seals were in use in Mesopotamia; the cylinder seal is a peculiar type not likely to be invented independently in two different countries; which country then owed it to the other? In Egypt the cylinder seal appears suddenly, and before very long goes out of fashion; in Mesopotamia it is the standard pattern for more than two thousand years. In Mesopotamia the natural and traditional writing-material is clay, which takes a seal-impression well; in Egypt it is paper, papyrus, on which you could not roll out an impression at all, and paper-using people would never invent the cylinder seal. Clearly, then, these seals are at home in Mesopotamia, and the Egyptians owed them, directly or indirectly, to the Euphrates valley.

Of course, comparative archæology has its dangers; one has to be sure of one's ground, and superficial resemblances may be utterly misleading. I remember a book which was meant to prove the Asiatic origin of Central American culture, and the main argument adduced was a stone carving on a Maya site representing an elephant with his *mahout*, a subject which could only have come from India. Unfortunately the author had relied upon a drawing made by a French artist, *not* an archæologist, who had done his best to make sense of a carving high above his head on the corner of a sculptured stone monolith, and the elephant and the *mahout* holding his goad were in his sketch unmistakable; but a photograph of the actual stone showed, equally plainly, a toucan, eminently an American bird, surrounded by demons. Very false conclusions have been arrived at by scholars who have compared the early painted pottery of different countries and, painstakingly analysing the designs into their simplest elements, have shown that these are identical and so have triumphantly claimed for the various wares a common origin. But the truth of the case is that those elements of design are necessarily simple and their possible range is very small—circles, squares, triangles and wavy lines, they are the basis of all design. What matters is, first—how they are elaborated and combined into patterns, and second—how they are applied to the pot, for the primitive potter is not concerned with inventing a design as such, he is producing a painted pot, and the shape of the vessel and the part of it to which his decoration is applied are just as much a part of the 'design' as are his painted lines. We are dealing with the products of human handicraft, and a purely abstract analysis which neglects the human element is bound to be wrong, Again, we may be misled by too confident an assumption of knowledge. At a great many sites in Palestine, Syria and Asia Minor there has been found painted pottery of a sort long familiar to archæologists as the ware characteristic of

PLATE XIX

Inlaid gold coffin for viscera
Tomb of Tutankhamen

(*See p.* 85)

PLATE XX

Inlaid wooden toilet-box
from a grave at Karanog

The 'tomb chapel' over
the entrance of a tomb
at Karanog, with its
brickwork undisturbed

*(By courtesy of the Trustees of the University Museum, Philadelphia)*

*(See p.* 88)

Cyprus in the Bronze Age. When therefore it occurred in excavations on the mainland it was regarded as proof of commercial relations between the mainland site and Cyprus, and since the chronology of the island was reasonably well established this 'imported' Cypriote pottery was unhesitatingly used as evidence for date. We found vast quantities of the ware at Atchana in the Turkish Hatay and I was quite prepared to accept the conventional view; but at Atchana we had independent dating evidence and after a time this evidence convinced us that while in the upper levels in which it was found it was indeed contemporary with what was found in Cyprus, examples of it coming from lower levels were a hundred and fifty years older than the earliest known in the island. Finally it became clear that this 'Cypriote' pottery was not by origin Cypriote at all but an import from Asia Minor which became so popular in the island that it drove all the old native wares off the market; when it occurred in Palestine or Syria it was again an import, but there it could not be dated by Cypriote chronology and is not necessarily a link with Cyprus at all.

Sometimes the link is by no means obvious. One winter at Ur we found deep under the royal cemetery, and quite distinct from it, a series of graves of a sort we had never seen before. The attitude of the body was unparalleled in later times, the pottery forms and the shapes of the stone vases were new to us, and the burials were marked by the presence of tumblers made of lead, a metal scarcely ever used in the royal cemetery. Now some years ago, at a place called Jamdat Nasr, nearly two hundred miles away to the north, there were found remarkable clay vases with designs painted in red, black and buff, and with them clay tablets inscribed with the oldest writing known in Mesopotamia, writing not by conventional signs but by pictures. Recently we discovered in a deep pit at Ur fragments of this painted ware, and with them a few bits of plain red pottery of a sort not reported from Jamdat Nasr, and not otherwise known at Ur. In one of our new graves that winter there was a red pot. Of course I had already my ideas as to the date of Jamdat Nasr, and as to the date of the graves, and they seemed to me to agree; but the red pot was further evidence. I stated in my report that though no fragment of Jamdat Nasr painted pottery and no scrap of Jamdat Nasr picture writing had been found in or anywhere near the graves, yet these were certainly of Jamdat Nasr date. When we were back in London we started to clean a pot from one of these graves which was so thickly encrusted with earth and salts that nothing of its surface was visible; as the dirt came off there appeared the geometrical patterns painted in black, red and buff of the authentic Jamdat Nasr ware. The link was an indirect one, but the comparative method was justified in its results.

I have talked of the 'date' of Jamdat Nasr; it was a loose expression and perhaps I ought to retract it, certainly not to let it pass without a warning. The archæologist can re-create a great deal of human history; he can bear witness to its vicissitudes, trace the progress of civilization, define the life of a city or of a nation by periods arranged in true historical sequence; but in the absence of written records we cannot fix dates. We are always being asked 'When did such and such an event happen?' we may know very well at what point in a sequence it occurred, but we cannot express our answer in terms of years. There is no empirical method of attaining such knowledge. The stratification of the soil on an ancient site does not go by mathematical progression; if each of the first three feet represents a hundred years it does not follow that ten feet equal a thousand; they may stand for four hundred or three thousand years. The archæologist may for his convenience talk in round numbers, but he is not really thinking in numbers at all, and if asked for dates he can only reply that he does not know. As we pass back, then, from history, which depends largely on written records, to pre-history, the archæologist's peculiar sphere, we have to accept periods instead of dates, and racial movements instead of the exploits of individuals; it is an impressionist picture painted with a broader brush, but it is not necessarily less true.

Written history tells us nothing about Britain before 55 B.C., and then deals only with the invasion of an island which we should suppose to have been inhabited by barbarous savages. Archæology can tell us of British kings in the south and east civilized enough to mint their own coins with dies modelled after the famous gold pieces of Macedon; by imports from the iron-workings of Hallstatt in Hungary, by the forms of bronze tools and weapons, by clay beaker cups, by megalithic monuments, it can trace trade relations with the Continent and the invasions of Continental tribes, can follow the shifting of the population as the older

PLATE XXI

Part of a log coffin of the Bronze Age from a Scandinavian
peat-bog showing the body with all the garments preserved

(*See p.* 90)

(See p. 92)

PLATE XXII

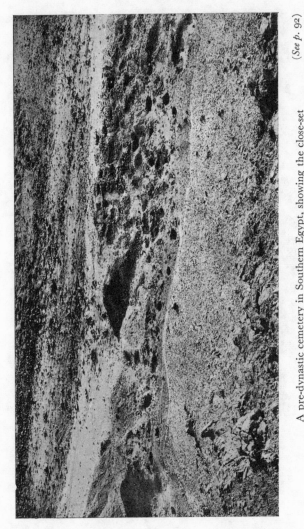

A pre-dynastic cemetery in Southern Egypt, showing the close-set grave-hollows in the sand

(By courtesy of the Department of Antiquities, Egyptian Government)

elements gave ground before the new-comers, can re-create in broad lines the beginnings of England. Nearly all that we know of Roman Britain, its topography, its economic conditions, the life of its people and the organization of government, is due to excavation; history has supplied little more than the skeleton. In *Puck of Pook's Hill* Kipling gives a picture of the Roman Wall as vivid as if he were describing life on the North-West frontier of India in the nineteenth century; the Roman writers have nothing to say about that great rampart which defended Britain from the Picts, nothing about the hot springs of Bath, or the villas of the Isle of Wight, but for every detail Kipling could quote the authority of the spade.

Here somebody might raise an objection. If, where periods have to serve instead of dates, archæology can still present so complete a picture, why was it stated a little while back that the archæologist's aim is an exact chronology? Really there is here no contradiction. From the stratified remains on your site you may work out the whole sequence of the development of an ancient community and describe its character in each successive phase; it is a valuable piece of work. But that community did not exist in a vacuum, it was one unit in a world of men; and if you are asked, what was the rest of the world doing? at any one stage of its advance was your community blazing a new trail for mankind or was it left behind in a backwater by more cultured nations? you cannot answer because you don't know the date of that stage. Someone in your community brings in a new technique; but the same technique is practised in some other land; which really invented it, and which learnt it from the other? Unless you can date the invention in each country you cannot rightly give credit to either. The value of an exact chronology is that it brings your community into its proper relation with the world of which it was a part, so that the isolated record takes its place in the ordered history of man.

## Chapter IV

## Grave-Digging

I HAVE DEALT HITHERTO WITH THE EXCAVA-
tion of buildings and what one can hope to
learn from them, and I have, I trust, made
it clear that most of the information which we
thus acquire is based either on the actual fabric
and ground-plan, or upon contents which in
themselves may have but little value. In the
ruins of a temple there may, with luck, be
statues and inscriptions, in a private house
such odds and ends as the last inhabitants did
not trouble to carry off; but if you go into a
museum and look at the antiquities collected
there, you can be sure that the vast bulk of
them were found not in buildings but in graves.

All over the world, and at most periods in the
history of each part of it, a belief in some kind
of life after death has induced man to place in
the graves of his dead things which may minister to the needs of another world; conversely,
from the fact that a grave contains such objects,
we can deduce that there prevailed a belief in

a future life. I am not speaking of such very personal things as decency would naturally leave to the corpse, the pin that fastens cloak or winding-sheet, the ring on the finger, the amulet worn in life about the neck, nor again of such things as might be considered mere offerings to the memory of the dead, the sword by the warrior's hand, the toy with which the child played and none other must play, the wreaths of flowers which are our modern expression of sad respect. 'Grave furniture,' to use an archæological phrase, is something far more definite than this, and answers to far more definite ideas.

The Greek placed on the dead man's mouth a coin to pay Charon his fare for ferrying him across the river of Death. The Egyptian might take with him a copy of the Book of the Dead to prompt his memory so that he might give the right answers to the gods or demons who held the gates of the under-world and cross-examined all who would pass through. In Mesopotamia vessels of food and drink provide sustenance for the long journey which the dead must undertake, and during one period these vessels are stacked on a boat made of bitumen, implying that the journey must be made by water. But the journey is not everything, there

PLATE XXIII

"Cleaned for photographing" (See p. 92)

Two pre-dynastic Egyptian graves with skeletons and objects in position

*(By courtesy of the Department of Antiquities, Egyptian Government)*

PLATE XXIV

Plaster cast of a wooden harp with copper cow's head attached, Ur

(See p. 95)

is the whole life of the next world, and because
it is difficult to imagine life otherwise than in
terms of that which we know, it is assumed that
man's occupations and needs hereafter will be
very similar to what they have been in the past
—the next world is a continuation of this.
Whatever, therefore, a man used and required
in his lifetime he will use and require after
death. The woman takes her spindle, her
needle, her mirror and her cosmetics, the
jeweller his balance and weights, the carpenter
his saw and chisels, the soldier his weapons of
war. The king must be provided with a goodly
sample of his pomp on earth: the viking leader
is laid in his barrow on the deck of his beaked
galley with all his gear about him; the Sumerian king has not only his treasure of gold and
silver, alabaster, lapis and bronze, but the
bodies of his slaughtered court to bear him
company and to minister to him in his new
sphere of royalty; the Pharaoh, in the rock-
hewn labyrinth of his tomb, had such provision
for his splendour that the grave of Tutankhamen, one of the most insignificant of Egypt's
rulers, found intact, has astonished the whole
world with its riches (*see* Plate XIX). It is not
surprising, then, that the archæologist derives
most of his material from the cemeteries of the

old world, and that what he there finds illustrates not only the beliefs and burial-customs
of the past, but also its everyday life.

Yet it must not be supposed that such a
wealth of objects and information is easy to
come by—that it lies in the ground just waiting
for the 'Open Sesame' of the spade; only too
often the excavation of an ancient cemetery is
a most disappointing task.

Legend says that when St. Patrick landed in
Ireland one of the natives showed him a round-
topped tumulus or mound and explained that
inside it was the body of a king lying on gold
heaped half a spear's length high. The saint
promptly dug into the grave and found the
gold, and in gratitude transferred from Pur-
gatory to Paradise the soul of the old pagan who
had thus provided funds for the propagation
of the Faith. The fact that so much gold was
buried in the tomb could not have been hid,
and would not be forgotten; when a new race
enters the land, or a new religion takes the
place of the old, the superstitious fears which
guarded the treasure lose their force and the
tomb is looted. Even without such a change,
avarice may prove stronger than piety. At Ur
we can trace in the soil of the great cemetery
the tunnels by which thieves made their way

down underground to the royal tombs when the whereabouts of these were still definitely known, perhaps marked by chapels built over them on the ground surface. Of all the tombs of the Pharaohs in the Valley of the Kings at Thebes only one, that of Tutankhamen, was overlooked by the robbers. And the robbers were early at work. We actually possess the written minutes of a Commission which was appointed by the Pharaohs of the XXth Dynasty to inquire into the wholesale plundering of those very tombs in the Theban Valley. Nor was such plundering confined to the wealth of kings. Of the ordinary rock-cut tombs of Egypt 99 per cent have been looted in antiquity and most of the remainder have been spared only because it was known that their contents were not worth the risk and labour of breaking into them; from the plundered graves the modern archæologist may hope to recover objects which the old thieves overlooked or deliberately discarded; in the rare cases where he comes upon a tomb intact he cannot help indulging in high hopes, but sober experience warns him beforehand that in all probability there is little to reward him there. At a place called Karanòg, in South Egypt, I excavated a large cemetery dating to the beginning of the Christian era, and secured a wonderful collection of objects belonging to the then scarcely known Meroitic civilization, but amongst them all not one thing in precious metal. The graves (*see* Plate XX [b]) were chamber-tombs cut in the firm Nile mud, with a sloped passage leading down to the doorway. In nearly every case the brick wall that blocked the door was intact; but at the back of the grave there had been a pit, down which libations for the dead were poured, and the robbers had simply got into the pit and burrowed a hole through into the chamber, a hole, perhaps, only big enough for a man to put his arm through. But that small hole was enough; the thief knew exactly where each object of intrinsic value had been placed. We, entering by the door, would find everything apparently undisturbed; the painted clay vases, the bronze bowls, the glass bottles, and toilet-box of wood inlaid with ivory (*see* Plate XX [a]) were all in their places, the body stretched out orderly and in peace. Then one would see, beyond the head, the jagged hole in the wall of grey mud; two or three fallen beads by the neck would show how the string had been snapped and the necklace snatched away; the right arm might have been bent up and back and a finger had been torn off for the sake of a gold ring; and if there had been any other object of precious metal (and its place then would surely have been near the head) it, too, had gone and left no trace. All the thefts had been committed by men who knew precisely what and where their booty was, and one can imagine that the sexton of the graveyard took careful notes of every funeral and made a very handsome profit on his inside information.

On the whole, therefore, whether it be a question of the Bronze Age tumuli of the British Isles, of Egypt's rock-cut shaft and gallery tombs, of the earth graves of Mesopotamia, or the bee-hive tombs of Mycenæan Greece, the archæologist must content himself with the leavings of older and less scientific plunderers, and will rarely find the treasure-house untouched.

But this is not all; apart from robbery there is the question of soil and circumstance.

In an Egyptian tomb cut in the living rock, absolutely dry and protected from the air by the sand which seals it almost hermetically, there is little to bring about decay. Woodwork may be shrunk and warped, will have lost much of its substance and be light and brittle, but it is generally still there, and the bedsteads and the chests, the wooden coffin and the figures carved in wood have suffered small damage from the passage of 3,000 years; even cloth preserves its nature, and the linen sheets of the bride's trousseau buried with her are still soft and strong, though yellowed by age, and could almost be used to-day; while such things as copper and bronze have undergone only surface change. From the peat bogs of Denmark the digger may unearth a coffin made of a hollow tree-trunk, and find in it the body of some old Bronze Age warrior, with his clothes of wool and leather discoloured but uncorrupted (*see* Plate XXI). In the graveyard of Ur, where, perhaps, only a layer of matting protected the dead man and his furniture from the damp and salt-laden soil, all these fragile things decay; of wood there is left but a patterned stain on the smooth face of earth, a paper-thin film grained in white and grey which can be seen and photographed but which a breath will make to vanish; copper and bronze may be reduced to a shapeless mass of green corrosion, and silver to a purplish powder; even the bones may have mouldered away, leaving only the teeth to show that here was a man; it is an irony of nature that our teeth, which decay so painfully while we live, stop decaying at our death, and outlast all the rest of us! Where an ancient people practised cremation instead of interment there may be even less to find, for the personal ornaments which survive on a buried body were often burnt with it. In the richest cremation-grave we ever discovered at Carchemish, that of a prince, apparently, who may have died in about the year 604 B.C., we found in the urn, mixed with the blue and grey splinters of calcined bone, a quantity of gold ornaments which must have adorned the dead man's dress; if they had not been actually flung upon the pyre they must at least have been put in the urn while the gathered ashes were still hot, for half of the delicate work, a unique treasure of archæology, had melted and run into shapeless drops of yellow metal. It is true that a cemetery will, as a rule, yield far more objects than will the buildings of a town, but, at the same time, we can only hope to recover but a small proportion of what the mourners put into the graves.

The method of digging graves must, of course, vary with the nature of the graves themselves. In Egypt a pre-dynastic graveyard consisted of shallow pits or troughs dug into the sand along the desert's edge; scrape away the modern surface of wind-blown sand

and the circles of greyer filling will betray the position of every burial—at least to eyes trained to see (*see* Plate XXII). For shaft-graves, again, the sand and gravel must be scraped away, and the rock exposed into which the square pit was hewn, and its outlines will show up at once, and then it is merely a matter of clearing out the rubbish from the pit until, thirty or fifty or perhaps a hundred feet down, the door is reached which leads into the tomb chamber. I have already explained how the Hittite graveyard at Yunus, near Carchemish, was located by the deep-rooted weeds growing in clumps out of the hard gravel soil; there we could dig where surface indications gave away the whereabouts of graves underground. At Ur we must needs dig uniformly over a wide area, for there are no surface signs, and the graves go down one under the other to varying depths, so that to-day a great excavation nearly eighty yards long and sixty wide and as much as forty feet deep alone testifies to the eighteen hundred graves which our notes record.

Coming to the actual work, the first principle of grave-digging is that nothing be moved. The excavator's record in notes, photographs and drawings must show every object in its original place (*see* Plate XXIII). This may

PLATE XXV

The carrying-chair of Hetep-heres, restored

The arm-chair of Hetep-heres, restored
*(By courtesy of the Boston Museum of Fine Arts)*

*(See p.* 98)

PLATE XXVI

(See p. 99)

The gold lion masks of Shub-ad's sledge exposed in the ground sound rather like morbid curiosity, or like mere method run to extremes for its own sake, but it is not: perhaps very little information will result from this careful detail, but a great deal *may*, and where everything has to be learnt the excavator cannot afford to neglect any evidence whatever from which knowledge may afterwards be gained, even though it has no obvious bearing at the time. So he will plot in the position of the grave, measure its depth in the soil, and then proceed to deal with its contents.

To keep objects in their original place is not always easy. Their condition is often such that you can scarcely touch either them or the earth round them without a disaster. In the case of burials set close together in the soil, where even the outline of the individual grave is difficult to define, one does not always know to which grave a given object may belong; an outlying vase, for instance, discovered while one grave is being dug, may prove to be part of the furniture of another not yet found; and though a wrong attribution might not seem so very important a mistake, it does matter, not for sentimental reasons, but because it might upset a whole system of chronology. Then, again, it is possible that some offerings were put into the grave-shaft while it was being filled up with earth, and so lie not on the same level as the grave but right above it; unless these are very carefully noted, their association with the grave will be lost, and, incidentally, the evidence for that particular custom will also pass unnoticed. So one tries to recognize as soon as possible the grave's existence, and from that moment begins specially careful work.

One of our richest graves at Ur, that which contained the famous golden helmet, was located by the discovery of a copper spear-head sticking point upwards in the earth. The soil was cleared from round it, and there came to light a length of thin gold tube which adorned the top of the shaft; below this there was a hole in the ground left by the wooden shaft itself when it turned to dust. We followed the hole downwards, and it led us to the grave, against the corner of which it had been leaning when the earth was thrown back into the pit; with this forewarning we were able to trace the entire outline of the grave before we started to lay bare its contents, and so could record in order all the offerings heaped and crowded round the coffin. In another case, a simple hole in the ground was found, and then a second; something unusual about their shape seemed to call for special treatment, and accordingly plaster-of-paris was poured in to fill up the void which decaying wood had left: the result (*see* Plate XXIV) was a complete plaster cast of a harp whose substance had long since vanished (except for the copper bull's head and the shell plaque which decorated the front end of it and were later found sticking to the plaster), and thus the first hint that we had of a grave's presence also enabled us to preserve the best object in it before we knew what it was—in fact, before we really knew that the grave was there. One has to look out for all such little things; for the thin powdery white streak which represents the matting that once lined the pit, for the holes in the soil where once were the upright wooden ribs of a wicker coffin, for the rim of a tall clay vase standing in the grave and not crushed flat by the earth's weight; on encountering any such thing the well-trained Arab pick-man will stop his work and report to the foreman the likelihood of a grave; then the pick will give place to the knife for careful work, and the excavator will get out his note books and his measures (*see* Plate I).

The clearing of a grave may be a long job. The mere removal of the earth so that the objects stand out well enough to make a good distinct photograph will require time and patience, especially as none of them may be moved in the process, and many may be very delicate or actually broken into pieces which only the earth holds together more or less in shape. In the case of the simplest grave the excavator's notes will give the attitude and direction of the body—sometimes a very important point, for there has often existed, as there exists to-day, a ritual determining such things, and that ritual may decide a period, a race, a religious belief; then there will be a drawing, or notes, giving the position of all the objects, including such details as, for instance, the order in which beads of various sorts were strung around the neck or arm; obviously a necklace is much more interesting if it is re-strung in its original order, and tells us more about the fashions of dress than would an arbitrary arrangement of beads collected promiscuously from the grave; but to obtain that the excavator may spend painful hours stooping or lying over the body as he cuts and blows away the earth so delicately as to leave the loose beads undisturbed. Then there will be measurements and measured drawings of the individual objects, and each of these will be marked with a number corresponding to that

PLATE XXVII

The body of Queen Shub-ad's sledge, restored

(*See p.* 100)

PLATE XXVIII

(*a*) The skeleton cleaned for photography

(*b*) The skeleton, waxed and shrouded, being undercut so that it
may be turned over on to the padded board

Removing a skeleton of the Flood period

(*See pp.* 101–102)

in his notes, so that subsequently the entire
tomb-group can be reconstituted for exhibition
or for study. But the labour required for noting
an ordinary grave may be enormously increased
when there are delicate objects in bad condition
or where there is material for reconstructing an
object which itself is broken or decayed; few
people, looking at such an object in the glass
case of a museum, realize what it cost to get it
there.

A fine example of the patience which goes
to the salving of an antiquity is given by the
tomb of Queen Hetep-heres, found by Dr.
Reisner close to the Great Pyramid at Gizeh.
In a walled-up recess behind the rock-cut
chamber in which stood the empty stone coffin
of the mother of King Khephren, the pyramid
builder, there lay a mass of decayed and
powdered wood and bits of gold plate, and
scattered over the floor were tiny figures cut in
gold, hieroglyphs which had been inlaid in the
wood and had fallen out as that crumbled to
dust. Had these just been gathered up they
would have been a pretty illustration of the
elaborate fashion in which the royal furniture
of Egyptian kings five thousand years ago was
adorned, and that would have been all. As it
was, the excavators cleared the chamber

laboriously square inch by square inch, recording the exact position of every tiny fragment:
they spent 280 days working there, took
hundreds of pages of notes and more than a
thousand photographs.   From three bits of
wooden frame and one panel, shrunk to a sixth
of their original size, but preserving traces of
the joints, tenons and mortices, they were
able to reconstruct a unique object, the carrying-chair of the queen (*see* Plate XXV [a]), the
gold hieroglyphs, assembled according to the
position in which they lay on the floor, formed
groups which could be arranged so as to give
sense, proper texts which decorated the upright
panels of the chair, and the chair which was
built up with new wood and the ancient gold
was an exact replica of the vanished original.
From the other remains of gold and wood the
same painful methods recovered an elaborate
arm-chair (*see* Plate XXV [b]), a jewel-box and
a bed; but after all had been removed from the
tomb the work of reconstruction took Dr. Reisner's men two whole years.

A somewhat similar piece of furniture was
the sledge-chariot of Queen Shub-ad, found at
Ur.  Quite unexpectedly there appeared, standing upright in the earth, a gold lion's mask
about four inches across, below which was a sort

of beard made of bits of shell and lapis lazuli
inlay, the latter loose and ready to fall at a
touch, so that they had to be secured at once
with hot wax. A second similar head was found
a little to the right, and a third equidistant on
the left (*see* Plate XXVI); cutting away the soil
between them we found, an inch or so further
back, a strip of mosaic, tiny squares and triangles of shell and red stone, also loose, but
forming a more or less straight line; clearly all
these had been attached to a wooden background which had entirely disappeared, and
were the decoration of an important object.
Higher up and further back another strip of
mosaic came to light and another row of gold
heads, this time much smaller and in rounder
relief, heads of lions and bulls; then on each
side vertical bands of mosaic in white and blue,
and more strips at right angles, running back
into the unexcavated soil. We put forward
various theories as to what the object could be,
a throne or a chest, but the main problem was
what to do with it. Since everything was loose
in the earth, and nothing was on the same plane,
it was necessary to remove one part before we
could get at the next, and the danger was that
thereby the design of the whole thing would be
lost. It was obvious that whatever the shape

had been, the woodwork had been crushed by
the weight of earth, and any one measurement
might be deceptive; only a very elaborate
system of measurement could possibly suffice
for a restoration. Each strip of mosaic, however
imperfect, was solidified with wax and muslin,
and by a multiplicity of notes and scale drawings its exact position in relation to every other
fragment was fixed, and then it was lifted out,
and the way cleared for getting back to the
next bit of ornament. The far side of the
chariot was of course approached from behind,
and we had to be on the look-out for bands of
black powder, the bitumen in which the shell
and lapis mosaic had been set, and as this far
side had collapsed inwards, and everything
stood askew, the bands were not easy to recognize or follow, and we had to determine how
much of this angle was original and how much
due to accident; I cannot say that our field-
notes were as voluminous as Dr. Reisner's, but
they ran to a great many pages before the last
bit of the chariot decoration had been removed.
When, from all the measurements taken, a restoration of the chariot was worked out on
paper, the total margin of doubt was found
to be only just over half an inch; it was possible to build up a new body in modern wood

PLATE XXIX

(*See p.* 103)

Digging out tablets at Ur

They are at once packed in sand in tin boxes

PLATE XXX

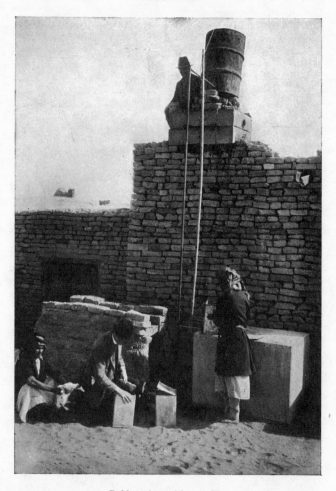

Baking clay tablets at Ur
The tins are being put in a furnace heated by vaporized oil from the
reservoir on the house roof

(*See p.* 103)

and set in it the old inlay and be sure that this was, within that narrow margin, a faithful reproduction of the original which had decayed to nothing four thousand years before (*see* Plate XXVII).

It was by a similar process that the gold and mosaic lyres from the cemetery at Ur were preserved, and the copper statues of cattle from al 'Ubaid; these had been made of thin metal hammered over wood, and the wood had gone to dust and the copper was crushed and broken into small fragments, and when unearthed was so soft that much of it could be scraped away as powder by the finger; nothing but paraffin wax and muslin would have held them together for transport. Wax is an extraordinarily useful thing in archæological work, and it has the great advantage of being simple to use. In the case, for instance, of the skeletons of the people who lived at Ur just after the Flood: the bones were flattened by the weight of fifty feet or so of earth, and where they were not reduced to powder were splintered to atoms, yet the bodies kept much of their shape, and were material invaluable for the anthropologist (*see* Plate XXVIII [a]). As much soil as possible was scraped and brushed away and then boiling wax was ladled generously over the skeleton

and the soil round it—the only difficulty was
that the earth was so damp, at the bottom of a
pit into which the sun seldom shone, that the
wax tended to form a skin over it instead of
sinking in—and then linen dipped in hot wax
was laid over the body and pressed well down
to fix it to the firm wax below. When the entire
skeleton was duly shrouded the earth below it
was cut away until it rested on three or four
slender columns and could be tilted over on to a
board covered with cotton wool laid alongside
to receive it (*see* Plate XXVIII [b]). The mass
of earth adhering to what had been the under
side was next cleaned off and the process of
waxing and shrouding was repeated; wholly
encased in waxed muslin, the body, hardly
more than an inch thick, but rigid, and so light
that it could be carried balanced on one hand,
was ready for packing and despatch to London.
There the upper coat of linen was steamed off,
the superfluous wax first scraped and then
washed away with benzene, the more discoloured bones bleached with peroxide of
hydrogen and hardened, if necessary, with
cellulose or gum damar, and the skeleton could
be shown exactly as it had been found, with
not one of its crumbled and splintered bones
disturbed.

In Mesopotamia a very different problem is presented by the written tablets which are so precious a part of the archæologist's spoils. Very often they are of unbaked clay and, buried in damp soil, have become as soft as cheese; softer, because their material is more homogeneous, than the earth which clings to them. It would be impossible to clean them without obliterating the incised signs which give them their value; if they are simply kept as they are, they are likely to crack or even fall to powder, since the clay is generally impregnated with salt, and would certainly not stand the shocks of transport; moreover, it is important for the field worker to know as soon as may be what information they may give—dates, names of buildings or of kings, to guide him in his work. At Ur any lumps of clay looking like tablets are lifted from the ground still encased in their covering of earth, and are packed in metal boxes filled with clean sand (*see* Plate XXIX); after they have been left for a few days to give the clay a chance to dry, the boxes are put into a rough-and-ready kiln heated by vaporized crude oil (*see* Plate XXX) and are baked until the tins are red-hot and the clay is turned into terra-cotta. Then the tablets are taken out; their colour may have altered, which matters little, but they are hard and strong; broken bits can be stuck together, the faces can be cleaned by brushing without any risk to the legibility of the characters (*see* Plate XXXI); no inscription, however fragmentary, can be overlooked, and its preservation is assured.

The work that one does on an object in the field is only preliminary, just what is necessary to remove it in safety and to keep its component parts together; the preparation of it for exhibition is often a far more complicated task, and can only be undertaken in a museum laboratory where proper facilities exist and chemical processes can be carried out. If the excavator is not qualified to do the work of repair himself, he must at least have some knowledge of how that work will be done, and will plan out his own part accordingly, as otherwise the measures he adopts to preserve his object may seriously interfere with its restoration. In fact, field treatment ought to be reduced to a minimum, so as to leave the laboratory expert with a free hand; at the same time the nature of the object may, as I have shown above, call for treatment involving no small amount of labour in the field, and the archæologist's first duty is to preserve.

## Chapter V

## The Use of Archæological Material

IN DESCRIBING THE METHODS OF SALVING
antiquities, I have emphasized rather the
importance of individual objects, and while
the excavation is actually in progress the
archæologist's attention is necessarily devoted
to each individual object in turn; as soon as it
is over he has to consider his discoveries
collectively, and what were museum exhibits
become units in a series out of which history
has to be made. We have been dealing with a
cemetery which presumably contains a large
number of graves; possibly we know the
approximate date of the earliest and the latest
burials, or one of them; in any case the cemetery
must have been in use for a considerable length
of time and therefore ought by its contents to
illustrate the modifications of culture which
took place during that time; very likely there
were no dates known at all when the dig began,
and the objects from the graves are the only
material we possess for the history of a long

period; how then is the archæologist to use his material?

Remember that as we go further back into the past, and our knowledge becomes more scanty, we have to deal in bigger time units; for archæology a century is a very short span, but a century then may have seen as many changes as a century now. The digger might lump together all that his graves have produced and say, quite fairly, that the collection as a whole illustrates a period of perhaps three hundred years; but in that case no single age within that three hundred year limit is correctly illustrated by the assembled objects. English life in 1650 was very different from what it was in 1900. A visitor from Mars seeing a great collection of English domestic objects, costumes, etc., ranging in date from 1650 to 1900, but all mixed up together, could get a general idea of a moderately high level of civilization, but could not picture what the setting of life was like at any particular date; if the things were put in historical order our Martian, assuming that he were reasonably intelligent, could not only visualize each period but could trace the course of invention and evolution throughout three centuries. That is precisely what the archæologist tries to do.

Where inscribed documents are found the history produced by digging may be extraordinarily detailed. At Meroe, in the Sudan, Dr. Reisner excavated a number of pyramid tombs which had escaped the notice of less methodical diggers; inscriptions showed that they were the graves of Ethiopian kings and queens. Now for a short time, about the seventh century B.C., Egypt was ruled by Ethiopian Pharaohs; their names were recorded, but nothing was known as to how this conquering dynasty developed in its original southern home nor what happened to it after it was again driven out of Egypt, nor by what process there evolved out of it the Græcised royal house of Candace which ruled Ethiopia in the days of the apostle St. Philip. Dr. Reisner was able to put all his tombs in chronological order and to work out the genealogical tree of the entire family; as the result of a single excavation a complete chapter of ancient history could be written for the first time, and the growth of a civilization which at one time dominated Egypt could be traced in detail. One can see how in this remote corner of central Africa there long persisted the primitive culture which in prehistoric days had been that of the lower valley of the Nile, how it was brought up against historic Egypt and re-acted to the more advanced civilization of the North until up-to-date organization enabled the Ethiopians to conquer their degenerate teachers by force of arms (*see* Plate XXXII). One can see how African inconstancy was unable long to hold what brute force had won, how the Negro love of foreign novelty made Ethiopia welcome Greek art, and spread an Alexandrian veneer over the essential barbarism of the Sudan; from the pyramids of Meroe, each reflecting in its furniture the contacts of the moment, there emerges the psychology of a race as well as the politics of many of its generations.

But supposing that there are no written records to define the order of our discoveries, what then? Then the archæologist is thrown back on his own resources; he has to deduce the order from the facts which he has observed and it is on the fullness and accuracy of his notes that the value of his results will depend. In my last chapter I remarked that the attribution of a pot to the wrong grave might upset an entire system of chronology; that is perhaps putting the matter strongly, but it is quite certain that unless the attributions are generally correct no chronology can ever be worked out. But it is not a question of tomb-

PLATE XXXI

(b) After being baked and cleaned

(a) As found

Clay tablets from Ur

(*See p.* 104½)

PLATE XXXII

(*See pp.* 107–108)

From the Pyramid tombs at Meroe
Objects showing the influence of old Egyptian and of Greek art
on the Merotic

*(By courtesy of Boston Museum of Fine Arts)*

groups only; every point in which one grave differs from another may prove to be evidence for relative dating, and must be brought into the argument; because nothing is known nothing must be neglected.

Where the number of graves is large, and the objects from them are numerous, it will generally be possible to recognize with tolerable certainty an earlier and a later group. In some classes of objects there are sure to be signs of development of technique, of the gradual conventionalizing and degeneration of ornamental motives, of the evolution of vase types, and extreme instances of any such process may be taken as dating evidence for particular graves. Sometimes this modification in the contents of the graves may correspond with their position in the cemetery, and it will be clear that the latter expanded in a regular fashion, either along a line or outwards from a centre, and then the plan of the cemetery will become the first basis of classification. Or the evidence may be more direct, as in the great cemetery at Ur, where very often the graves lie one directly below another in a series which may number half a dozen separate burials; obviously the lower grave must in every case be older than the upper, and wherever the

series of superimposed graves is fairly long the
lowest of all is likely to date fairly early in the
period represented by the cemetery as a whole,
and the topmost is likely to be reasonably late
in the same period. This is the one certain
fact on which all future argument must be
based.

The archæologist first analyses in tabular
form the sum of his field notes; in parallel
columns he will have the number of each
grave, its depth, character, direction, and all
its contents symbolized by type numbers—
then he can proceed to make his comparisons.
Taking first the score or so of graves which by
their position at the bottom of a series he knows
to be relatively early, he compares their contents, and will probably find that they have a
good deal in common—that the same types of
clay vessels and the same forms of weapons or
tools appear in many of them. Then, taking
the score or so of late graves, he may find again
that there is a certain similarity between them,
but that the pottery types of the early graves,
and the metal forms, do not re-appear, or re-
appear seldom, in the late graves, while the
forms which characterize the latter are wanting
in the early group. If he can establish that fact
he is on fairly sure ground. Assuming that his

two groups do represent approximately the beginning and the end of his cemetery period, he will go on to examine in the light of their contents the rest of his graves. Graves which contain only forms regarded as early will be added to the first group; those with some early types mixed up with others about which nothing is as yet known will provisionally be classed together as marking a step forward in time; those in which early types are out-numbered by unknown types will be attributed to the next phase of advance. Similarly with the later groups; according as types agree wholly or in part, graves will be attributed to the last or to the penultimate phases of the period which the graveyard represents. Perhaps in this way a third of the graves may be placed in what is hoped to be a chronological grouping, and two-thirds will be left over as containing types still indeterminate. These provisional results must then be checked. The graves of the group supposed to be the earliest but one, how do they lie in the ground? Does their depth in relation to the other graves justify our theory? Do the other contents, beads, gold ornaments, cylinder seals and so on agree with the evidence of the pottery and the bronze tools? If they do, we can assume that we are on the right track, and then the types of vessels and tools found in them, but not in the graves of the earliest group of all, can be taken as characteristic of their period, and can be used for classifying other graves in which they occur, but the earliest forms are not found at all. Gradually, fresh groups are formed at the expense of the undefined residue of graves left between the early and the late groups, and with fresh evidence arising from each new classification, that undefined residue is in time reduced to nothing, and the whole cemetery is classified in a series of groups of graves which follow a really chronological order and illustrate a rational process of evolution; we still cannot date our periods in terms of years, but we can follow the changes of fashions in things, and therefore in the habits of people, and can attribute any object, by its style, to a definite place in a historical sequence.

Then begins a further correlation. On building sites we have found the remains of houses lying one above the other, each level producing its harvest of broken clay pots, copper utensils and what not. Comparing these with what our cemetery has given us, we may be able to connect various building strata with the sequence-periods of the graves; then for each

phase we shall have something of the conditions of living as well as the habits of burial;
if, in the building strata, there are ruins of
temples, we can add elements of religious ritual
and belief.

Just as, in the process of excavation, the
archæologist requires the help of the architect
for the reconstruction of his buildings, and of
the epigraphist for the reading of his inscriptions, if such be found, so, too, a measure of
team-work is necessary for dealing with the
mass of material of all sorts which excavation
provides for the reconstruction of social life.
The complaint is often made that archæological
publications are intolerably dull and consist of
masses of undigested detail which cannot
possibly interest anyone other than an archæologist; the answer to this is that the book is
not meant for general consumption; conscious
that he cannot himself exhaust his subject, the
excavator, while putting his own conclusions
on record, offers to other specialists the whole
of the material evidence on which those conclusions are based, and invites further study;
it may be long before the last word has been
written, but in the end there will emerge
from that chaos of disconnected facts the
history which justifies everything. The graves,

for instance, will have produced a number of human skulls and skeletons; the anthropologist will take charge of them, and from their physical characteristics determine the racial connections of the original people and perhaps trace the advent of new stocks, and the relative dating for that advent may coincide with the appearance of new fashions in weapons or pottery; the evidence of disease, arthritis, abscesses in the teeth and so on, will help to explain life conditions, and the setting of broken bones or marks of trepanning will illustrate the surgical knowledge of the period. Figures in stone or clay, drawings on pots or engravings on metal may give some idea of the looks and dress of the people; remains of cloth—sometimes only the impression preserved on metal of cloth whose substance has perished—will show their skill in weaving, and spindle-whorls, loom-weights and combs will illustrate its process; the constant recurrence in the graves of a long pin lying near the shoulder and parallel with the bone of the upper arm will prove that the outer garment was an unshaped and unsewn shawl or cloak wrapped round the body under one arm and fastened by the pin over the other, a brooch under the chin will mean a shaped gown open at the neck, the remains of a belt will add to the picture which, with knowledge of materials and some idea of styles, we can begin to form. Preserved in their original order, bracelets, necklaces and head-dresses reproduce rather than suggest the past. The elaborate head-dresses worn at Ur by the court dames of the period of the royal tombs are by now familiar—in the Sargonid age, about 2300 B.C., they have given place to simple ribbons of gold; had these been purchased in the market they would have told us nothing, but found in position they show how two long plaits with gold coiled about them were brought from behind the ears and fixed one above the other across the forehead. Such early Sumerian pictures of men as we possess show them gener-ally clean-shaven, sometimes with long hair, and it was long supposed that the latter must be of a different race. In the graves of the royal cemetery the men commonly wear a head-band made up of two lengths of gold or silver chain and heavy beads of lapis and gold secured behind by a string; now this can only be an early form of the modern Arab 'ageyl', or head-rope, which holds in position the head-cloth worn over the clean-shaven skull; we can fairly argue that the old Sumerian was shaven and wore a head-cloth. But in one grave, whereas the body had the normal head-band, quite apart in a corner of the coffin there was a heap of light brown dust still keeping the texture of hair, and on it lay a plain gold fillet and in it were two spiral hair-rings of gold; on certain occasions the shaved Sumerian wore a wig, just such a ceremonial wig as is represented in the wonderful gold helmet of Mes-kalamdug found in the same cemetery. Then in graves, again, we find articles of the toilet, tweezers, *kohl*-sticks for painting the eyes, *kohl*-bloxes and whole sets of unguent-vases in alabaster (these in Egyptian tombs) and in Mesopotamia cockle-shells with paint of various colours; we feel that we know the looks of these long-dead folk, something, too, of their tastes and ideas. We have actual specimens of their handicrafts, objects in metal, stone and clay, which not only fulfilled ascertainable needs and served as a means of self-expression, but may indirectly guide us to fresh knowledge. The geologist will try to trace the sources from which were derived the raw materials, often imported from abroad, of the manufactured goods; foreign connections and trade routes become manifest. Etruscan graves in Italy, Crimean barrows, graves in Syria and Hungary show how the traders in Baltic amber pushed their business into the far

South; the tools and weapons of the royal
cemetery at Ur are of bronze, containing a
certain percentage of nickel, and as the only
ore known to contain nickel in that proportion
comes from Oman, on the Persian gulf, we can
safely assume that it was from Oman that the
Sumerians of 2700 B.C. derived the metal for
their foundries, while the lapis lazuli, which
they employed so freely for ornaments, came
from the Pamir mountains, N.W. of India.
Below the deposit of sand left by the Flood we
found two beads of amazonite, a green stone
for which the nearest known source is in the
Nilghiri hills of Central India, or in the mountains beyond Lake Baikal—and at once there
is called up the astonishing picture of ante-
diluvian man engaged in a commerce which
sent its caravans across a thousand miles of
mountain and desert from the Mesopotamian
valley into the heart of India.  Bones found in
the midden-heaps of houses, or scattered on
their floors, will tell the naturalist what breeds
of domestic animals were kept, what wild
animals were hunted and eaten; the dried
contents of store-jars or pots of offerings will
show what grains and what fruits were grown
and used for food, while arrows of special types,
fish-hooks and net-sinkers, hoes, ploughshares,

sickles and grindstones illustrate the manner in which the hunter and the farmer played their part.   If written documents be forthcoming with which the epigraphist can deal, much more may be learnt of social organization and of positive chronology, but even without that the comparison of the contents of different strata ought to bring out the main vicissitudes of a city's life, as well as the slower processes of development and decay.

But here one must strike a warning note. However fruitful in discoveries an excavation may have been and however well the digger has performed his multifarious tasks he must never think that he can say the last word on the subject.   He has been working, let us say, on a town site whose well-defined strata cover a long period of time, and in the light of them he can work out a rational scheme of history.   But what is true of his town need not be true of a quite near-by neighbour; the political influences that affected one may have left the other untouched.   If, as is generally the case, he has dug only part of the site, his evidence is partial and further digging might have modified his conclusions; or, again, his stratification, seemingly complete, may by some accident omit an entire cultural phase, either because the people of that phase did not occupy the part of the city which he has dug or because a wholesale clearance of the site by the builders of the succeeding phase has destroyed the evidence that once was there. Thus at Tell Tay'inat in the Hatay an eighth-century Syro-Hittite palace is built directly on the top of ruins of the fourth millennium B.C.; the same is true of Tell Halaf in northern Mesopotamia, where appearances did mislead the excavators. If one relied upon the evidence of Ur one would conclude that the primitive al 'Ubaid period was of relatively short duration, seeing that it was represented by not more than five levels; but at Eridu, twelve miles away, sixteen temples have been found one above the other and all are of al 'Ubaid date! A single excavation is not likely to yield a complete or a continuous record, but by the time a number of sites have been dug the sum of the results worked out by the field archæologist and his collaborators will be a genuine addition to history. To-day we can read, as our grandfathers could not, the story, vivid and circumstantial, of civilizations newly unearthed and of epochs in man's experience which until recently were literally 'dark ages'; and realizing that of all this we have perhaps no contemporary written evidence, or

virtually none, some may have been inclined
to doubt its value, mistrusting the imagination
which seems to base so much on a few potsherds.
There must be imagination if life is to be
breathed into the dry bones of a dead civilization, but imagination has not been allowed to
run riot; the value of the 'few potsherds' as
documents for the building-up of history
depends, as I have tried to show, on the
scientific methods which the archæologist employs in his work; accurate observation and
faithful record are preliminary to any reconstruction.

The prime duty of the field archæologist is
to collect and set in order material with not all
of which he can himself deal at first hand. In
no case will the last word be with him; and
just because that is so his publication of the
material must be minutely detailed, so that
from it others may draw not only corroboration
of his views but fresh conclusions and more
light. Should he not then stop at this? It
might be urged that the man who is admirably
equipped to observe and record does not
necessarily possess the powers of synthesis and
interpretation, the creative spirit and the
literary gift which will make of him a historian.
But no record can ever be exhaustive. As his

work in the field goes on, the excavator is
constantly subject to impressions too subjective
and too intangible to be communicated, and
out of these, by no exact logical process, there
arise theories which he can state, can perhaps
support, but cannot prove: their truth will
depend ultimately on his own calibre, but, in
any case, they have their value as summing up
experiences which no student of his objects and
his notes can ever share. Granted that the
excavator is adequate to his task, the conclusions which he draws from his own work ought
to carry weight, and he is bound to put them
forward; if they are palpably wrong then his
observations also may justly be held suspect.
Between archæology and history there is no
fenced frontier, and the digger who will best
observe and record his discoveries is precisely
he who sees them as historical material and
rightly appraises them: if he has not the power
of synthesis and interpretation he has mistaken
his calling. It is true that he may not possess
any literary gifts, and that, therefore, the
formal presentation of results to the public
may be better made by others; but it is the field
archæologist who, directly or indirectly, has
opened up for the general reader new chapters
in the history of civilized man; and by recover-

ing from the earth such documented relics of the past as strike the imagination through the eye, he makes real and modern what otherwise might seem a far-off tale.

# Index of Proper Names